Good Kids/Bad Habits

Also by Charles E. Schaefer

Young Voices: An Anthology of Poetry by Children
Developing Creativity in Children
Becoming Somebody: Creative Activities for Preschoolers
Therapeutic Use of Child's Play
Therapies for Children
Childhood Encopresis and Enuresis
Therapies for Psychosomatic Disorders in Children
Therapies for Children with Common Problems
How to Help Children with Common Problems
How to Influence Children
Group Therapies for Children and Youth
Handbook of Play Therapy
Family Therapy Techniques for Problem Behaviors of Children and
  Teenagers
How to Talk to Children About Really Important Things
Game Play: Therapeutic Use of Childhood Games
Advances in Therapies for Children
Teach Your Baby to Sleep Through the Night
Children in Residential Care: Critical Issues in Treatment
Innovative Interventions in Child and Adolescent Therapy

Also by Theresa Foy DiGeronimo

AIDS: Trading Fears for Facts
Raising a Healthy Athlete
Your Premature Baby
Hooked on Exercise
College Admissions Through High School Sports

Also by Charles E. Schaefer and Theresa Foy DiGeronimo

Toilet Training Without Tears
Teach Your Child to Behave
Help Your Child Get the Most out of School
Raising Baby Right
Winning Bedtime Battles

Good Kids/**Bad** Habits

Charles E. Schaefer, Ph.D.,
and
Theresa Foy DiGeronimo, M.Ed.

Prince Paperbacks, New York

Although the authors have worked closely together to write *Good Kids/Bad Habits*, the first-person "I" who speaks to you throughout the book is the voice of Dr. Schaefer.

A Prince Paperback book. Published by Crown Publishers, Inc., 201 East 50th Street, New York, New York 10022. Member of the Crown Publishing Group.

Random House, Inc. New York, Toronto, London, Sydney, Auckland

Prince Paperbacks and colophon are trademarks of Crown Publishers, Inc.

Manufactured in the United States of America

Book design by Jennifer Harper

Library of Congress Cataloging-in-Publication Data
Schaefer, Charles E.
   Good kids/bad habits/Charles E. Schaefer and Theresa Foy
DiGeronimo.—1st ed.
   Includes index.
   1. Habit breaking in children.   2. Child rearing.   I. DiGeronimo,
Theresa Foy.   II. Title.
BF723.H32S33   1993
649'.64—dc20   92-7437
                                                       CIP

ISBN 0-517-88003-2

10 9 8 7 6 5 4 3 2 1

First Edition

For our own good kids who taught us quite a bit about bad habits:
Karine and Eric Schaefer and
Matt, Joey, and Colleen DiGeronimo.

Contents

Acknowledgments   ix

Chapter 1   Creatures of Habit   1

Chapter 2   Habit Busters   11

Chapter 3   Interest Boosters   23

Chapter 4   Thumb and Finger Sucking   31

Chapter 5   Nail Biting   45

Chapter 6   Hair Pulling   55

Chapter 7   Stuttering   65

Chapter 8   Teeth Grinding   75

Chapter 9   Masturbation and Self-Touching   85

Chapter 10   Tics
              (Shrugging, Blinking, Squinting,
              Shoulder or Head Jerking,

Grimacing, Head Shaking or
Nodding, Nose Wrinkling)   93

Chapter **11**   Other Common Habits
(Nose Picking, Knuckle
Cracking, Finger Tapping,
Foot and Leg Wiggling,
Cheek Chewing)   103

Index   109

Acknowledgments

We would like to thank our agent, Faith Hamlin, and our editor, Irene Prokop, for their continued and enthusiastic support.

Good Kids/Bad Habits

1

Creatures of Habit

You're probably reading this book because your child has a bad habit that's driving you crazy. Before you despair, let me assure you that annoying habits are quite common in childhood. To get an inkling of just how common childhood habits are, take a good look at any large group of children—at school or on the playground or in your own neighborhood. Look closely for the things they do absentmindedly while they're playing. Some pick their nose while talking to friends; others crack their knuckles while waiting for a turn at bat; some suck their thumb while playing in the sand; and surely you'll see nail biting, hair twirling, foot tapping, and self-touching. When children first do these things, they're usually very much aware of what they're doing. It takes practice to get the knack of knuckle cracking; picking the nose serves a practical purpose; sucking a thumb, twirling hair, and self-touching feel good and reassuring; and foot tapping relieves tension. But now as you watch children practice these behaviors you'll see they are almost involuntary and automatic—they have become habits.

A habit can be defined as a learned behavior that's repeated so often it becomes automatic and persistent. Although we tend to notice only bad habits, the word *habit* itself implies neither good nor bad. A habit can be "good" if it's something we encourage our children to develop; habits like buckling seat belts, looking both ways before crossing streets, saying please and thank you, and brushing after meals are habits we want our children to develop.

A habit can be benign if it's something we can safely ignore because it's not harmful. Habits like Johnny Carson's persistent necktie fiddling or George Bush's hand gesturing are ingrained, automatic movements that are a part of the person's character and certainly don't need to be encouraged or broken. Childhood habits like occasional foot wiggling or quiet humming fall into this category and can usually be safely ignored.

Then there are "bad" habits, which are the focus of this book. Bad habits are ones that are persistently embarrassing, self-injurious, or annoying. These habits should be broken to protect the physical and emotional well-being of children.

Roots of Habits

What causes habits? It seems logical that if we could find the exact cause, we could focus on that and stop the habit from forming. Unfortunately, there doesn't appear to be one definite root for most habits. Instead, habits are the result of a combination of factors that most commonly include imitation, a need for anxiety or tension relief, and/or positive reinforcement.

Imitation

Children are notorious copycats. If you watch them closely you may notice that they imitate the way you tap your fingers on the table while thinking. They buckle their seat belts only if older siblings do. They'll even spit on the ground with gusto if their friends do. These are learned behaviors that children intentionally mimic because they want to look and act like other people.

Other forms of imitation are more subtle. You probably know small children who have picked up some of their parents' mannerisms—a crooked smile, a raised eyebrow, or a particular stance. These behaviors are copied by children on a subconscious level, but they're learned by watching parents very closely.

Actions or behaviors that are copied, either consciously or unconsciously, can become lifelong habits. Ted, for example, who started cracking his knuckles because his older brother did, found himself twenty years later unconsciously cracking loudly at an important job interview. Meg, who twirled her hair like her mother, now has trouble controlling her habit as she teaches her fourth grade class. Ted and Meg know that what often begins as a learned behavior through imitation can end as a persistent and bothersome habit.

Tension Relief

How does your body respond to tension? Some people get headaches, others feel butterflies, and some even have heart palpitations. Still others fall back on old habits that help them physically discharge their nervous feelings. Among others, foot and finger tapping, nail biting, facial tics, hand and face rubbing, and throat clearing are very common ways of relieving tension and anxiety. These tension relievers are always evident in my college classes as I hand out the final exam. All around the room, students are tapping, jiggling, rubbing, coughing, and biting nails. I know these students will act the same way when they move on to their next exam and still again when they venture out into their careers.

Initially these behaviors seem soothing and so children use them repeatedly to face day-to-day tensions. Soon, however, they become automatic nervous habits that are practiced continuously even when there's nothing to be nervous about. My students practice their nervous habits just to pass the time as they wait for class to begin. The root of these behaviors is in tension relief, but the habit continues even when the tension is gone.

Positive Reinforcement

Positive reinforcement is anything that encourages us to repeat a behavior because it is followed by a pleasant event. Smiles and praise encourage babies to walk. Promises of candy or toys can encourage children to behave. Attention encourages bad habits.

Attention in the form of nagging, hollering, and threatening is often used in the attempt to break bad habits. If a parent says "Don't bite your nails" every time the child's hand wanders to the mouth, that child is getting more attention each day than he or she could have ever hoped for without the nail-biting habit. Even a negative response can be reinforcing and can encourage repetition of a behavior in a child who is starved for attention.

❖ ❖ ❖

These three roots of habit formation—imitation, tension relief, and positive reinforcement—are the most common causes of habit formation. They instill lifelong habits in people without regard to race, sex, or even hereditary predispositions. Although the process is quite normal and the resultant habits are in no way signs of personality disorders, some habits can and should be broken in childhood before the thinly woven strands of habit become reinforced steel cables.

Why Bother?

We should break children's bad habits for the same reason we should encourage good ones like buckling seat belts and brushing teeth: to protect children's well-being. Unfortunately, most bad habits bother parents and children only after the behavior is deeply ingrained and is noticeably embarrassing, self-injurious, or annoying.

Embarrassment

Children are quite sensitive to ridicule. Once the habit of thumb sucking or nose picking is formed, for example, school-age children will find themselves being laughed at by young friends or siblings. Because true habit takes away personal control, a child's sobbing vow of "I'll never suck my thumb in class again" won't end the thumb sucking or the teasing it causes.

Embarrassment isn't something young children (or most adults, for that matter) can just shake off. An embarrassing habit can cause emotional and social problems. Seven-year-old Jake, for example, was in the habit of jerking his head to the side. He'd often use this jerking movement, called a tic, while doing homework, watching TV, or playing video games. His mom and dad found the habit annoying, but they didn't think much of it until they realized its side effects.

After several weeks of watching their son become increasingly withdrawn, Jake's parents finally coaxed him to explain why he didn't want to go to school anymore and why he quit the soccer team. They found that the kids in Jake's class and on his team had made a game of mimicking his tic and he now realized that sometimes he didn't even know he was doing it until someone mockingly called attention to it. Jake's habit made him the target of childish cruelty and the consequences were serious: His schoolwork was suffering, his self-image was being damaged, and his previous enjoyment of soccer was being sacrificed to fear of ridicule. Sometimes the painful side of childhood habits isn't noticed until they lead others to laughter.

Physical Harm
In addition to the emotional and social damage that can be caused by bad habits, physical damage can result as well. Habits like hair pulling, teeth grinding, cheek chewing, nail biting, and sometimes thumb sucking negatively affect children's health, and should most certainly be broken in early childhood.

Thirty-eight-year-old Laura remembers pulling strands of hair from her head as she sat in her kindergarten classroom. She would carefully separate and select one long strand and pull. Then she'd examine the hair for its texture, color, and length. The practice seemed innocent enough at that time, but today Laura wears a wig to hide the permanent bald spots she's created by pulling one strand after another for years. Her habit is self-injurious, and should have been broken when it first began in childhood.

Annoyance
Some bad habits aren't emotionally or physically disruptive, but still should be broken because they're annoying to other people. Ted's knuckle-cracking habit, for example, will certainly annoy potential employers during his job interviews and perhaps cost him a good job. Habits like eye blinking, finger tapping, and foot jiggling also fall into this category of annoying behaviors. Like all habits, once they're established, they're tough to break. If you feel your children repeatedly practice a particular behavior that would detract from the professional or personal image they might want to project in adulthood, now's the time to intervene.

Why Not Ignore?

Many adults still wrestle with their own bad habits because the behaviors were ignored during childhood in the mistaken belief that they would eventually be outgrown. A careful look at the process of habit formation makes it clear that the more a behavior is repeated, the more likely it is to become involuntary, automatic, and persistent. Once the behavior is tightly held in habit's grasp, ignoring is completely ineffective because the children are generally unaware of what they are doing. Ignoring allows the behavior to be continually repeated.

If you choose to try ignoring as a habit-busting strategy — beware. If it doesn't work (and it most often won't), the habit will become more firmly entrenched with each passing day. By the time you realize your child needs a more active approach to the problem, habit strands that were once loosely woven will have tightened and become more strongly reinforced and more difficult to break.

Getting Ready To Bust Bad Habits

The habit-busting strategies explained in the following chapters will be most effective if you first take some time to set down a foundation that will give your children a secure and determined attitude toward the idea of breaking the habit. In the end it's your children who must want to stop the habit and who must work their way through the habit-busting program, so a positive attitude will take them a long way toward breaking their habits. The following guidelines can be used to encourage your children to beat the problem.

Modeling
Learning by imitation is called modeling. If you want your child to learn how to break a habit, you can help by modeling habit-busting strategies yourself.

"Do as I say, not as I do" has never been an effective parenting technique. In the case of bad habits, it is especially counterproductive. If you and your child share the same bad habit, you're setting your child up for a difficult and probably futile habit-busting experience if you continue to practice the habit yourself.

Let's say, for example, that you bite your nails. Because you've learned the hard way that nail biting is an unhealthy, embarrassing, and often painful habit, you'd like to spare your children the same experience by stopping the habit before it becomes firmly implanted in their behavior pattern. Using yourself as an example of what *not* to do, you encourage your children to stop biting, but you continue to nibble. This mixed message asks children to turn against their natural inclination to imitate you. The results will most certainly be disappointing.

If you'd like your child to break a bad habit that you yourself don't have, you can still find ways to model the habit-busting program with your child. Watch yourself closely over a twenty-four-hour period; surely you have some annoying or unhealthy habit that you could get rid of. If, for example, you cross your knees when you sit, tell your children that because that position is bad for circulation, you plan to stop doing it by using the same habit-busting strategies they're using. Then you can monitor each other's progress through the program.

We teach best with actions, not words, so if you're plagued by a bad childhood habit, now is the perfect time to join forces with your child and break it together.

Public Commitment
If your children are three years or older, you can motivate them to follow the habit-busting strategies explained in this book by having them tell friends and relatives about their decision to break the habit. Imagine in your own life how much easier it would be to pass up the cheesecake at your neighbor's party if you had already announced that you were trying to lose weight. This kind of public commitment makes it much easier to resist temptation.

In the same way, public awareness will give your children the push they may need to follow through on their good intentions. Knowing that grandma, grandpa, dad, and older siblings are watching their progress gives children an additional measure of awareness and motivation—both important components of habit busting.

Support

The purpose of public commitment is not to put pressure or shame on children with bad habits; it is to gather and sustain support. A good friend at the neighborhood party wouldn't use your diet announcement to ridicule, tease, or threaten you; she would stand by to encourage your efforts and praise your successes and coax you back to your diet when you fail.

You can give your children this same positive support system every day during the habit-busting period by using the following support helpers:

▶ Compliment commitment and determination.

▶ Remind your children of their past successes when they seem discouraged.

▶ Comment approvingly on any sign of progress.

▶ Console your children lovingly during setbacks.

▶ Keep your doubts and frustrations to yourself.

The habit-busting experience shouldn't turn into a disciplinary war of wills between you and your children. Bad habits are most easily broken when you're both on the same side and working together in positive and rewarding ways. Modeling, public commitment, and support throughout the habit-busting process will give your children that positive base they need to hang on to. The six habit-busting strategies explained in the next chapter and used throughout the book will provide them with the specific techniques they need to bring them successfully to their goal.

Habit Busters

Once you realize that wishing and hoping won't make your child's bad habits go away, you'll need a concrete plan to break the habit reflex. This chapter will explain six strategies that I have used successfully over the years: shaping, trigger identification, self-awareness, response prevention, competing response, and monitoring. Each strategy is explained here in detail and then, in later chapters, is applied to the process of breaking specific habits.

Shaping

Habits form gradually, almost unnoticeably. Stopping them works the same way—in very small steps. This gradual approach to changing behavior, called shaping, moves children toward their goal one step at a time. As Mark Twain once observed, "Habit is habit, and not to be flung out of the window by any man, but coaxed downstairs a step at a time."

Most parents turn to habit-busting strategies when they've run out of patience. "That's it!" they tell me. "I'm not going to let my child be the butt of school jokes anymore. What should I do to make sure that this never happens again?" Sadly, I have to tell these well-intentioned parents that there is no quick-fix remedy for bad habits. The process of habit busting is a slow one that bit by bit reduces the number of times children practice their habit behavior, until finally it's eliminated or changed to a more desirable one.

Don't expect your children to stop their bad habits tomorrow—you'll both be disappointed. Strive first to cut down on the number of times the habit appears each day. A change from twelve instances of nail biting to ten is progress and deserving of applause, not despair. For example, instead of instructing nail biters not to bite their nails "anymore," parents might first encourage them to stop nibbling during homework time. This is a confined period when parents are usually nearby to keep an eye on progress, praise successes, and call attention to setbacks.

When children are able to complete a homework assignment without nail biting, then a new goal can be set. The habit might then be prohibited during TV viewing time. Later, with the support of the teacher, it can be restricted during school hours, and then in ever-increasing chunks of time, until the habit is licked.

Behavior shaping is an integral component of habit formation and an equally vital factor in habit busting. Shaping alone, however, will rarely break a well-established habit. It should be used along with the other techniques explained in this chapter, which will give your children greater awareness of their habit, suggest substitute activities, and offer a reward-and-penalty incentive system.

Trigger Identification

Many habits are practiced only in specific situations or places. The strategy called trigger identification will help you identify when and where your children most often use their habit behavior. By avoiding, changing, or slowly eliminating the trigger, you can work to break the association your children have made between that time, place, or situation and the habit itself. If, for example, your child masturbates most frequently while watching TV, the amount of time spent masturbating can be reduced most easily by limiting TV time. Because shaping is vital to the habit-busting process, you shouldn't try to end the habit by completely eliminating the trigger right away. As you're working with other strategies to get rid of the bad habit, you can slowly remove the triggers that provoke the habit.

Habit triggers shouldn't be ignored during the habit-busting proccess. If you try to change only the habit behavior without giving equal attention to its associations, these triggers will continually tempt your children and sabotage their efforts. If the parents of the masturbating child use all the recommended habit-busting strategies but neglect trigger control, their efforts at shaping, self-awareness, and monitoring will fall flat as long as the child still spends much unsupervised time in front of the TV. The child will fail this test of self-control time and time again because TV viewing is too strongly intertwined in the habit. It too must be changed.

Self-Awareness

Quite obviously, you have no motivation to tighten the leaky faucet in the bathroom if you don't know it's dripping. In fact, not noticing and therefore not fixing the problem is the reason a little drip can become a steady flow. In the same way, your children have no motivation to stop their bad habits if they don't know they've got them. Like the dripping faucet, it's exactly because an action goes unnoticed that it becomes strongly established. That's why awareness is so important in the habit-busting process.

The self-awareness techniques recommended throughout this book help make children aware of their habits in consistent and noncritical ways. In the past you may have tried to make your children aware of their habits by yelling reminders like "Stop biting your nails!" "Don't suck your thumb!" or "Get your finger out of your nose!" This tactic does make children suddenly aware of what they're doing, but at the same time, the shame, embarrassment, or anger it causes leads them to seek the security of the habit even more.

Each habit calls for a unique set of awareness techniques, but most often the process is always the same. Children are instructed to perform the habit intentionally and repeatedly to get a better understanding of what is actually happening, how it feels, and how it looks to other people.

Thumb suckers, for example, sit in front of a mirror while intentionally sucking their thumb. They watch how they move their hands, mouth, and lips. They do this every day to imprint the image in their mind. Then when their parents call attention to the habit later in the day, the children have a clear mental picture of what they're doing, how they look, and why their friends might call them "baby." In a similar way, teeth grinders concentrate on the physical movements of their habit. After intentionally grinding their teeth, they describe to their parents exactly what happens to their jaw and neck muscles, which side of the mouth they grind, whether they use a back-and-forth or sideward motion, and how this tension makes them feel.

In addition to these intentional self-awareness tactics, you can continue to encourage awareness at other times of the day by gently and kindly interrupting the habit when it occurs. Rather than falling back on the old method of yelling out a warning, establish a "secret" communication system. You might agree to interrupt the habit by placing your hand firmly on the child's shoulder. Or you can devise a code message like "Hey, bud, how are ya doin'?" The goal of this interruption is to stop the habit behavior, increase the child's habit awareness, and at the same time avoid ridicule or embarrassment.

Awareness training may initially cause some children to practice their habit more frequently. If this happens, don't worry. Consider it similar to the process of cleaning a closet — the effort will make the area messier before it finally looks cleaner, but unless you jump in and do it, the job will never get done. Awareness training is an absolutely necessary part of habit busting; a behavior can't be changed until it's brought to the conscious level and recognized.

Response Prevention

As its name implies, response prevention stops children from practicing their habit. Nighttime thumb sucking, for example, can be prevented by taping a wooden tongue depressor to the inside of the elbow joint. This prevents a sleeping child from getting the thumb anywhere near the mouth. Response prevention helps break habits because every time habit episodes are prevented, the urge to practice the behavior weakens.

Don't feel you need to force-feed prevention tactics. Because they're not generally subtle, you need your children's full cooperation to use them successfully. So if your child with a leg-wiggling habit doesn't want to put a weight on the leg while doing homework, skip response prevention and use the other strategies discussed in Chapter 11.

Competing Response

A competing response is a behavior or activity that children can use to replace or ease the frequency of their bad habits. A competing response either can take the place of the habit behavior, making it inconvenient to practice the habit, or can switch the child's focus to something else to delay the habit; this reduces the number of times it's performed each day.

Competing responses that give children a substitute activity also give them a sense of control over their habit. If, for example, children agree to chew gum rather than suck their thumb, the chewing action makes it difficult to suck and at the same time gives them an opportunity to make a personal choice to chew rather than suck, which in turn reduces the frequency of the habit and encourages self-control. The competing response best suited to each habit is explained in the following chapters.

Relaxation techniques can be used as competing responses to ease tension triggers. If your children practice nervous habits such as nail biting, stuttering, knuckle cracking, or any other bad habit that becomes more frequent under stress, relaxation exercises can be used to take the place of the nervous habit. Once your children replace their bad habit with the new relaxing habit, they will have gained a lifelong stress response that will help them deal with tension in a healthy way.

The relaxation exercises described below can be substituted for bad nervous habits. When you and your children zero in on what stressful situations prompt the bad habit, you can help your children practice relaxing before they are in the situation; this can head off a habit attack. If, for example, your monitoring chart (see page 22) shows that the habit most frequently occurs when the household is busy and hectic (often just around suppertime when your attention is on cooking, the telephone is ringing, and you're flying around straightening up the house), remind your children to start the relaxation exercises *before* the pace gets harried. This anticipation and preparation puts the children in charge and makes it clear that they have the power to substitute a positive activity for a negative one.

Not all relaxation techniques work for all people. Give your children time to practice each of the following and choose the one that feels most comfortable. Then be sure your children practice the exercise every day so that when they feel stressed they can easily and automatically cut off the bad habit with this competing response.

Relaxation Exercises

Thought Control: Thought control is a method of stress management that's based on a very simple premise: When your children talk to themselves, they should say something nice. Teach them that when they hear themselves muttering resentful, angry, or self-pitying thoughts, they should change them. Encourage them to change those negative thoughts to loving ones; help them recall times when they were successful at something, or happy about an activity or accomplishment. While they're doing this, tell them to smile. Smiling is a natural tension reliever that makes it almost impossible to feel tense. As your children learn to fight back against tension, they'll find that the way they talk to themselves is very important in the way they react to the source of the stress.

Deep Breathing: The body needs extra oxygen to fuel its stress response, so your children can reduce the stress they feel by maintaining control of their breathing pattern. To help your children avoid or stop the rapid breathing that often accompanies stress, teach them this technique:

▶ Take a deep breath from the bottom of your stomach. Feel it fill you with warm air.

▶ Breathe in as you silently count to five.

▶ Let the air go. Don't push it out. Let it go gently to the count of five.

▶ Do this sequence two times in a row.

▶ Then breathe regularly (rhythmically and comfortably).

▶ Deep-breathe again after you have let a minute or two go by.

▶ Repeat this deep-breathing/regular-breathing cycle two or three times, or as often as needed until you find the tension has passed and your breathing can return to a natural and comfortable pace.

Guided Imagery: Guided imagery allows your children to retreat to an inner world where they can feel safe and relaxed. This approach is based on the belief that imagining a positive experience can stop, interrupt, or prevent a stress reaction.

To help your children practice guided imagery, tell them to think of a place that they find totally relaxing. The place should be completely nonstressful—no angry friends, no arguing parents, no fear of failure. They might, for example, imagine themselves at a carnival where the lights are bright, the music is upbeat, the rides are free, and there's no one there except your children and their friends. In this special place, nothing goes wrong.

Wherever your children decide to build their relaxing place—in the woods, at the park, by a lake, or in their own room—help them practice going there often. The more familiar they are with the details of the place, the more readily they will be able to imagine it when they feel tension coming on.

No one can feel tense and relaxed at the same time. So if tension is your child's trigger, relaxation exercises can short-circuit the habit behavior and replace it with a habit that provides recommended stress-control tactics that can be used into adulthood.

Monitoring

During the habit-busting period, help your child keep a daily record of the frequency of the habit behavior. A written record works to reduce habits in three ways.

First, careful monitoring gives children a sense of personal control over the situation. Once the behavior is charted and recorded, feelings of helplessness often disappear. The reason for this empowering force of monitoring isn't fully understood, but it works. Recording each time a child engages in a bad habit on the Habit Monitoring Chart on page 22 helps the child see the habit as a concrete, controllable action.

Second, monitoring helps parents and children find the triggers that surround the habit. Sometimes the trigger appears to be quite obvious, as in the blanket that sets a young child to thumb sucking, but monitoring will point out other aspects of the trigger that may not at first be so noticeable. Does the child seek the blanket more often when tired? hungry? unhappy? bored? The chart on page 22 leaves a space for you to note the time of day and the activity that preceded the habit behavior. After a week of monitoring, you may notice a pattern that shows a time and/or activity that sparks excessively frequent habit behavior. In most households, each hectic day runs into the next and these kinds of patterns and triggers go unnoticed until someone begins to chart the habit and record when and where it occurs.

Finally, monitoring gives you and your child a written record of progress. Because you'll be aiming for gradual change, milestones of progress can easily go unnoticed unless the exact number of times a habit is practiced is carefully written down. Your child will probably not notice the decrease from twenty-two to fifteen instances of hair pulling in a five-day period. But written down in black and white, this change is an undeniable sign of progress.

Make a few copies of the monitoring chart. Although successful habit busting can take anywhere from three weeks to three months, begin with a four-week supply of charts. Fill in the dates at the top of each. Then hang this week's chart in a place that is easily accessible and in full view of your child.

During the week, place an **X** mark on the chart *every* time you notice your child practicing the habit. If your child goes a full hour without practicing the habit, put a happy face or a star on the line next to that time period. The next chapter will explain how, in addition to marking progress, these **X** marks, happy faces, and stars can be used to motivate your children to want to break their bad habits.

If your child goes to school, you can ask the teacher to keep a schooltime chart, but you probably shouldn't expect it to be completely accurate. There are many other students, activities, and responsibilities that take a teacher's attention away from your child, so many instances of habit behavior will go unnoticed. Some teachers may even refuse your request to keep a schooltime chart, knowing their ability to do a competent job is limited. In this case your monitoring efforts will be restricted to at-home time. Although not ideal, at-home monitoring should give you enough daily time to motivate your child, point out triggers, and show progress.

Once you've digested the information in this chapter and have mapped out a plan for rewards and penalties as explained in the next chapter, you'll be ready to begin a program tailored specifically to your child's bad habit. If your child practices a habit not mentioned in a chapter title, be sure to read Chapter 11; there you'll learn how to apply the strategies to any other habit you'd like to change.

Habit Monitoring Chart

Directions: Put an **X** mark at the appropriate day and time when you see your child practicing the bad habit. Note the activity that the child was engaged in when the habit occurred. Put a star on the chart when your child passes a period of time without practicing the habit. At the end of each day, add up the **X** marks and stars and record the total.

Week #_____ Date_____

	MONDAY		TUESDAY		WEDNESDAY		THURSDAY		FRIDAY		SATURDAY		SUNDAY
Time	Activity	Time	Activity	Time	Activity	Time	Activity	Time	Activity	Time	Activity	Time	Activity
8:00___		8:00___		8:00___		8:00___		8:00___		8:00___		8:00___	
9:00___		9:00___		9:00___		9:00___		9:00___		9:00___		9:00___	
10:00___		10:00___		10:00___		10:00___		10:00___		10:00___		10:00___	
11:00___		11:00___		11:00___		11:00___		11:00___		11:00___		11:00___	
12:00___		12:00___		12:00___		12:00___		12:00___		12:00___		12:00___	
1:00___		1:00___		1:00___		1:00___		1:00___		1:00___		1:00___	

etc., through end of day

3

Interest Boosters

Don't be surprised if after a few days of habit busting your children announce, "I don't want to do this anymore." Although the six habit-busting strategies explained in the preceding chapter can break bad childhood habits, the process can be a slow one; without something to encourage their continued cooperation, children tend to forget their initial enthusiasm. The following system of rewards and penalties will help you motivate your children to stick with their plan to beat the habit.

Rewards

It's a basic law of human nature that we tend to repeat acts that bring us pleasure or recognition. So it naturally follows that if children are rewarded for trying to break their habit, they'll continue to try. Despite the logic of positive reinforcement, many of us first use penalties and punishments to keep our children on track.

When I ask parents to describe how they have tried in the past to break the bad habit, their methods almost always focus on negatives—taking away a privilege, restricting TV or play time, ridiculing, or scolding. Yet these same parents agree that children (and adults, for that matter) have a better attitude toward doing something that's difficult if there's something positive in it for them. So before using penalties (as explained later), give rewards a try.

There are two kinds of rewards: social and concrete.

Social Rewards

Social rewards are positive consequences that can motivate children to break a bad habit through the use of praise, recognition, approval, and attention. The following guidelines, adapted from our book *Teach Your Child to Behave*, will help you use social rewards in ways guaranteed to show the best results.

Be Specific: When you give your children social rewards, avoid using vague words like *terrific, good,* or *wonderful.* When people make such general evaluations they tend to exaggerate, and so the praise sounds false. Children are very much aware when they really didn't do what they're being praised for.

Zero in on and specifically describe the worthwhile behavior that you want to reinforce. Instead of saying, "That was great!" you might say, "I'm really impressed by the way you clenched your fists right now to stop yourself from biting your nails."

Also, be sure to praise observable actions, not the whole child. You don't want to damage your children's sense of self-worth by giving the implied message that they are "good" children only when they do what you tell them to. Rather than praise the child's total personality by saying, "You're a wonderful kid," praise the specific behaviors that you want to encourage by saying, "I can see you're trying to relax when you do your homework so you don't blink your eyes as often."

Give Immediately: It's best to give praise immediately. Offer a social reward while your child is in the act or just finished. As your child sits quietly at the kitchen table say, for example, "It's nice to see you sit through dinner without drumming your fingers on the table." Compliments offered the next day lose their ability to change behavior. So, although you may not yet be in the habit of giving positive attention to nonhabit moments, try to remember to use social rewards when you notice your children *not* practicing their habit.

Don't Mix Praise and Criticism: You can avoid spoiling the effectiveness of social rewards by staying away from comments like the following, which imply criticism:

"It's about time you stopped sucking your thumb."

"It's nice that you watched a TV show without biting your nails for a change."

"You finally got through a conversation without jerking your head."

Social rewards have been proven highly effective in changing children's negative behaviors into positive ones. It's these kinds of rewards that you should use first in your attempts to break bad habits. They can be offered anytime; they're not costly or cumbersome; they never need to be phased out; and your children will work very hard to get you to use them.

Concrete Rewards

Concrete rewards are tangible things or privileges, such as food, money, toys, or special activities that can encourage cooperation and motivation. When social rewards aren't enough to change your children's behavior, tagging them on to concrete rewards may do the trick. These rewards are given out according to "Grandma's Rule," which says: "When you do this, then you get that." You already use this kind of reward system when you say, "Eat your dinner; then you can have dessert," and "Clean your room; then your friend can come over." Now to discourage bad habits, you can add a consequence that says something like, "If you can go two hours without twirling your hair, I'll give you a package of stickers." Or, "If you practice your awareness exercises in front of the mirror for five minutes every night this week, you can have a friend sleep over on Friday night."

Obviously the best kind of reward is something your child likes, but this reward system shouldn't cost you a fortune. Small items that show you're aware of your child's likes and interests should work. Consider crayons and paintbrushes for budding artists, fishing hooks or lures for young fishermen, barrettes or headbands for young ladies. You might also find you can motivate your children with a surprise grab bag. Fill a bag with small, inexpensive items that your children like and let them close their eyes and draw one out each time they've passed a given time period without engaging in their habit.

Children ages six and older may not be swayed to continue the habit-busting program with small, dime-store items, but they will change their behavior for special privileges. Because it's difficult to dole out special privileges every night, you might try this token reward approach:

Before you begin the habit-busting process, offer your children a special privilege. Explain that an afternoon at the movies, a pizza party with friends, or something equally appealing to them can be earned by following the strategies you'll outline for breaking their habit. You might begin by requiring one full day of compliance to collect the reward, and then stretch the time period by an additional day every time a privilege has been earned.

Because special privileges aren't granted immediately, you may need to help your children make the connection between their behavior and these kinds of long-range rewards. You can do this by putting token rewards such as stars or stickers on their monitoring chart every hour they pass without practicing their habit. These stickers offer a simple and visual way to keep track of progress.

Eight-year-old Anna, for example, always asks her mother to play board games with her. So they worked out a reward plan by which Anna and her mother would play the game of Anna's choice if she could resist sucking her thumb from after school until bedtime on the following Tuesday. Anna's mother checked her progress every hour and put a star on the chart to praise her success and encourage her to continue. A half hour before bedtime, Anna proudly pointed out her complete column of stars and so her mother gladly cleared the kitchen table and sat down to play Anna's favorite game — checkers.

The next day, Anna will again avoid thumb sucking to earn

a reward, but this time the deal will be slightly different. Now Anna will need two habit-free afternoons to collect her prize. The habit-free time span will continually increase and the rewards will become smaller until eventually, with help from the other habit-busting strategies, Anna gains confidence in her ability to break her habit and no longer needs concrete rewards.

Evaluate Your Reward System

Keep track of how well concrete rewards entice your children to follow the habit-busting program. If the rewards you're using aren't working, don't give up this positive approach. Look for a more powerful reward or vary the rewards you offer so your children don't lose interest. Remember, the first steps in breaking a habit are the hardest ones, so they deserve very special attention.

When used consistently, social and concrete rewards will motivate your children to stick to the habit-busting process long enough to see positive results. However, sometimes children may become stubborn and refuse to continue the program despite your reward system; in this case you may need to use penalties as a negative consequence.

Penalties

Penalties are the most common disciplinary tactic used in most households, yet when it comes to breaking bad habits, they remain quite controversial. Because habits are performed on the subconscious level, it's difficult to say if it's productive to punish children for something they don't even realize they're doing.

Penalties are most appropriately used in this program to

motivate effort. If your children refuse to practice their self-awareness or relaxation exercises for five minutes, then you may be able to gain cooperation by taking away five minutes of playtime. Or if your children suck their thumb while you read them stories, you can remind them of their habit by stopping your reading until they stop sucking. These kinds of penalties avoid harsh scoldings, spankings, and angry responses that make everyone hostile and resentful and put an obstacle in the path of habit busting.

Although penalty suggestions are included in some chapters, always first try to gain your child's cooperation with rewards rather than punishments. And remember: Penalties alone will never effectively stop bad habits.

Enforcement Guidelines

Whether you use positive or negative consequences to motivate your children, there is an enforcement guideline you should always follow: Enforcement of consequences must be done consistently and immediately.

Be Consistent
When you offer a reward or penalty, make sure you are willing and able to carry through 100 percent of the time. You should not say you will take away TV viewing time, then give in when a favorite show comes on. Also, you can't impose penalties for uncooperative behavior one night and ignore the same behavior the next. These inconsistencies sabotage your efforts. In the same way, you should follow through on your promise of rewards. If you reward every hour your child avoids the bad habit on Monday but then ignore the good behavior on Tuesday,

you'll weaken your ability to change behavior with positive attention.

Give the Consequences Immediately
Promise consequences only when you're sure you can deliver immediately. Don't offer a reward that you don't have in the house. A package of stickers given as soon as you finish the final count-up of "good" hours on the monitoring chart will serve as an effective concrete reward. The promise of getting such a reward sometime the following day after you get to the store to buy it is a strategy that will lose its motivating impact if and when the reward lands in the child's hands. Also, don't say you're going to impose a penalty "as soon as your father gets home." Any delay such as "when I finish this report," or "when I get off this phone," or "when your grandma leaves" will diminish its power to persuade.

Interest boosters are an important part of the habit-busting program. Whatever bad habits your children are trying to break, rewards and penalties will help them keep going when they're tempted to quit.

CHAPTER 4

Thumb and Finger Sucking

Most children voluntarily drop the habit of thumb and finger sucking before the age of five. By this time, they have developed other sources of pleasure and security; peer pressure and fear of appearing "babyish" also encourage them to resist the habit. However, many thumb and finger suckers do continue the behavior well past their fifth birthday. Although these children no longer need or necessarily even want to continue sucking, the habit is too strongly established to stop without help.

The following information about how thumb- and finger-sucking habits are formed from infancy through early childhood should help you accept early sucking habits, prevent later ones, and break those already established.

INFANCY

Thumb and finger sucking undoubtedly comes from an inborn need. Sonograms commonly record fetuses sucking in the womb. Later infant sucking is an instinct necessary to survival—it assures the intake of nourishment. Beyond this instinctive need, infants find pure pleasure in the sucking motion. Although this urge begins to lessen between three and six months of age, by that time thumb and finger sucking may have already become a habit and so many infants continue the practice.

You should not try to stop an infant's thumb or finger sucking. The practice offers the baby peace and calm at a time when life must often seem hostile and overwhelming. You can, however, begin to prevent the practice from becoming habit.

Habit Prevention for Infants

Thumb or finger sucking can be limited by increasing a baby's feeding time to allow longer sucking opportunity. If you bottle-feed your baby, use a slow-flow nipple to extend the feeding time to at least fifteen or twenty minutes. If you nurse, allow your baby fifteen or twenty minutes at the breast; even if the breast empties, the extra time satisfies the sucking need.

When a baby is irritable, don't immediately try to hush the cries by plugging in the bottle, your nipple, or the thumb. Try first to find the cause of the distress. Maybe the baby is bored, ill, lonely, or tired. It takes more effort to remedy the cause of crying but it helps interrupt the baby's growing association between sucking and easing discomfort.

Lastly, you can ward off future thumb- or finger-sucking problems by introducing a pacifier in the first or second month of life. Research shows that the pacifier is less dangerous than thumb or finger sucking to the developing mouth because it exerts less pressure against the teeth and roof of the mouth. It's also easier to control the child's use of a pacifier and its eventual elimination.

These three methods of prevention can help keep an infant's natural sucking instinct from becoming a bad habit. But beyond these tactics, you shouldn't put undue emphasis on sucking because in the first year of life, sucking on thumb or fingers is healthy and normal.

TODDLERS (ONE TO THREE YEARS)

About 40 percent of toddlers suck their thumb or fingers. At this age, before permanent teeth erupt, the habit is still relatively harmless and socially acceptable. The practice also serves to help children through the transition from total parental dependence to independence; the comfort derived from sucking gives children a self-directed way of handling stress without looking to their parents for help.

Habit Prevention for Toddlers

Although you shouldn't try to break the sucking habit at this stage of the child's development, you can continue preventive efforts that weaken the sucking habit.

Many toddlers suck their thumb or fingers when they're bored. You can therefore reduce their daily sucking time by keeping them actively involved in play or games. Offer hands-on projects like clay molding and coloring that will keep their hands busy and their mind off their habit. If your children are in a nursery school, encourage their teachers to stay attentive to the habit and ask them to guide the child gently to another activity if they notice the thumb in the mouth.

PRESCHOOLERS (THREE TO FIVE YEARS)

About one-third of all preschoolers suck their thumb or fingers, but it's still too early to break the habit with a formal habit-busting program. At this age, before permanent teeth come in, there is still no danger of damaging the teeth or mouth structure by thumb or finger sucking. Also, most preschoolers can't make a lasting commitment to stop a behavior that brings them instant gratification. It is time, however, to fortify preventive strategies.

Habit Prevention for Preschoolers
You can help your preschoolers end their thumb- or finger-sucking habit by biting your tongue when you're tempted to say, "Get your thumb out of your mouth." As contradictory as it seems, nagging, shaming, and ridiculing can increase the strength of the habit. Some children use negative reinforcement to gain attention and so they will suck, hoping to be repri-manded. Others will retreat after a scolding to the security of thumb or finger sucking to calm their upset feelings. Still others will use their habit to win victories in their battle to achieve independence from their parents' control. The following pre-vention strategies work best with preschool children because they don't call undue attention to the habit.

Respond to the Cause: Use the monitoring chart on page 22 to record when your children most frequently suck their thumb or fingers. This information may point out a pattern of sucking that you can change. If your children suck their thumb when they're bored waiting for you to finish your housework, for example, you can change the pattern by either inviting them to help you complete the job or by offering a toy, puzzle, or crayons to keep their hands busy until you're done.

Perhaps you'll find that your children suck their thumb or fingers most often while waiting for lunch or dinner. In this case the habit may be a means of staving off hunger. Try changing mealtimes so the child has food before the sucking reflex kicks in.

Many children suck their thumb or fingers when they're tired. If your monitoring chart shows you that at the first sign of fatigue the thumb goes into the mouth, you should take a closer look at your children's sleep schedule. Maybe they need an earlier bedtime, or maybe they still need a nap or rest period each day. Bedtime thumb and finger sucking is an especially difficult habit to break and so it gets special attention in the habit-busting process. But while your children are still young, your best bet is to try to ward off the fatigue that sets the sucking into action.

Quite commonly children suck their thumb or fingers when they feel insecure. A new baby, a new house, a divorce, or even an argument with a friend can increase the use of the habit. You can help break this association by offering other forms of security like a bit of extra attention. Work to eliminate stress by keeping your home environment as calm as possible and by assuring your children that they are loved, understood, and accepted.

Use a Reward System: You can reduce the frequency of pre-schoolers' thumb or finger sucking by using a reward system. Although you shouldn't nag or scold your children about their habit, you can express your disapproval of it. Then consistently praise them when you catch them not sucking and withhold your attention when they do. If preschoolers are ignored when sucking and praised when not sucking, most will begin their own grass-roots effort to break their habit.

FIVE YEARS AND OLDER

Twenty percent of five-year-olds still suck their thumb or fingers. These children need an organized habit-busting program to stop the habit because the longer they persist in the habit beyond this age, the greater the risk of physical, social, and emotional damage.

Habit-Busting Strategies

To begin this program, you should engage your children's cooperation in the habit-busting process. Explain the following strategies that have helped other children end the problem in two weeks to three months. Then encourage your children to give it a try.

If your children refuse to cooperate or if stress-related behaviors like whining, fighting, or clinging continue for more than a week, stop the program. These children aren't yet emotionally mature enough to give up their source of instant gratification. In this case you should wait six months and try the program again — or you can ask a dentist to install the dental appliance discussed at the end of this chapter, which can successfully break the sucking habit in even the most resistant children.

Trigger Identification

You've probably noticed obvious patterns that tie your children's sucking habit into triggers like tiredness, boredom, or a particular comfort object like a blanket or doll. Now use the monitoring chart on page 22 to uncover the less noticeable patterns. For one full week before you begin the program, put an X mark on the appropriate space every time you see your child sucking. Also note the location and/or activity that accompanies the habit. The patterns that develop can help you break the habit.

For example, Mary's chart showed that her daughter, Kate, sucked her thumb most frequently while holding her stuffed bunny and watching TV. Whenever the child, the bunny, and the TV got together, the thumb went in the mouth.

After the triggers were clearly identified, Mary found there were several ways she could use this information to limit Kate's daily sucking time. She could restrict TV time and offer her daughter other toys and activities in its place. Or she could restrict the availability of the bunny by proclaiming that it had to stay in Kate's bedroom. It wouldn't be appropriate to eliminate the TV or the bunny completely, but by reducing the amount of time the two are available to Kate, Mary will gradually be able to lessen the daily sucking time.

Once the habit is controlled in a given circumstance, extend the restriction to another time or place. Because Kate also sucked her thumb during her evening story time, her mom extended the thumb-sucking restriction to this time of day after she was sure Kate could comfortably watch TV without her bunny or sucking habit.

Self-Awareness

Once you have identified the habit triggers, help your children become aware of their thumb sucking. Have them consciously suck their thumb or finger in front of a mirror for five to ten minutes, once or twice a day at set times. Such practice helps bring the habit under conscious, voluntary control and makes children more aware of when the sucking occurs, what it feels like, and what they look like when doing it. This repetitive practice also tends to make the sucking more work than pleasure. Vigorous sucking of the thumb or fingers for an extended period of time can be quite boring, and the pleasure aspect soon fades.

Awareness can also be increased with habit reminders. Reminders are anything that can be put on the thumb or finger to help children keep their habit-busting goal in mind. Fingernail decals help children resist the temptation to suck because sucking would ruin the decal. A manicure and nail polish may reduce a young lady's urge to suck. Boys may be willing to resist their habit to preserve a watercolor tattoo. Not only will reminders motivate children to keep their thumb and fingers out of their mouth, they serve as a constant reminder of the habit-busting program.

Response Prevention

When your children are aware of their habit, help them find gimmicks that will prevent them from sucking their thumb. Some children will agree to have a tongue depressor taped to the inside of their elbow joint; when they can't bend their elbow, they can't suck their thumb or fingers. Some children will willingly bandage their thumb or fingers to reduce the pleasure of sucking and to interrupt the involuntary and subconscious aspect of the habit. Kate keeps a winter mitten on the TV set; she says that when she puts on the mitten before watching TV, she doesn't have to worry about sucking her thumb.

Bedtime thumb and finger sucking is an especially difficult aspect of this habit. Even determined, self-motivated children find their thumbs wet, soggy, and sore in the morning. In this circumstance, response prevention may be especially helpful. Any of the above tactics will help reduce nighttime sucking, but taping a clean sock over the entire hand can be particularly effective. If your children are willing, cover their hand with a sock and then use adhesive tape to secure it to their arm. If the sock is still in place in the morning, they've mastered a major hurdle in the habit-busting process and have certainly earned a special reward.

Competing Response

Thumb and finger sucking are a form of oral addiction. As many cigarette smokers know, willpower alone usually isn't enough to stop the need for oral gratification. A substitute oral activity will ease the habit-busting process. Encourage your children to chew sugarless gum when they're in a situation that frequently promotes thumb or finger sucking. Kate's mom put a package of gum on the TV set and told Kate to take a piece before she turned it on. When Mary saw that Kate still seemed a bit uneasy sitting in front of the TV without her bunny and without sucking her thumb, she brought in a pile of coloring books and a new box of crayons and encouraged Kate to color while she watched cartoons. This arrangement worked well. Kate's bunny wasn't in the room, her mouth and hands were busy, and she wasn't tempted to suck her thumb.

Finding something else to do with the thumb or fingers is

another kind of competing response tactic. When Kate doesn't feel like coloring while she watches TV, she plays one of two thumb games. She hides her thumb from her mouth by tucking it inside her fist. Or, if her thumb wants to come out, Kate has learned to twiddle her thumbs to keep them active and away from her mouth. Kate knows she won't suck her thumb if it's busy doing something else.

Some children suck their thumb or fingers when they're nervous or tense. These children can stop their sucking re-action by practicing relaxation exercises that eliminate the stress trigger. The deep-breathing exercise explained in Chapter 2 is particularly appropriate for thumb and finger suckers because the breaths are taken in and out through the mouth. This exercise not only relaxes the body's response to stress but also offers a competing response by giving children some-thing else to do with their mouth when they are tempted to suck.

Also, the thought control and guided imagery exercises pre-viously explained can be combined to help children control this habit. Most children over the age of five are afraid that their habit will make other children laugh at them. Using thought control, they can remind themselves that they are now big and no longer want to look like a baby. When tempted to suck, they can tell themselves over and over again how grown-up they look without the thumb or finger in the mouth. While engaging in this internal dialogue, children can create a mental image that allows them to see themselves in full control of their habit and looking very grown-up. Help your children practice this mental dialogue and imagery so that when they feel stress or are in a situation that they've learned leads to stress, they can immediately begin their internal relaxation plan.

Rewards

Rewards can quite successfully help children control their thumb- or finger-sucking habit. Read over the information regarding rewards and penalties in Chapter 3 and then set up an incentive system that you feel is most likely to motivate your children to end this habit. A typical system follows this course:

The first step in setting up a reward system is to restrict your child's thumb or finger sucking in a particular place or situation and then immediately reward compliance. Kate, for example, agreed she would not suck her thumb while watching TV. Her mother warned that she would peek in every five to ten minutes during TV viewing time to see if the thumb was in Kate's mouth, and she would also inspect the thumb to see if it was wet or soggy. If Kate refrained from her habit during that period, she would put a star on her progress chart. On the first day, five stars earned Kate a new toy from the grab bag her mother had put together. On the second day, the process followed the same course but Kate needed seven stars to earn her prize. On the third day, TV time and story time were monitored and ten stars were needed to earn a reward, and so on each day until concrete prizes were phased out completely. Kate's mother always combined praise with the offering of stars and toys and so as the concrete rewards were slowly phased out, the praise continued the job of encouragement.

Penalties

In addition to giving rewards, you can weaken a habit by imposing a mild penalty each time you observe thumb or finger sucking during a restricted time. If Kate was found sucking her thumb while watching TV, her mom didn't get angry; she put an X mark on Kate's chart *and* turned off the TV for five minutes. If Kate sucked her thumb while listening to a bedtime story, Mary immediately stopped reading until Kate removed her thumb from her mouth. Kate's desire to avoid missing the TV show or the story motivated her to become more aware of her actions.

A highly successful penalty, tested as safe and effective and recommended by members of the American Academy of Pediatrics, involves the use of commercially available bitter-tasting liquids that are painted on the thumb or fingers. In one particular study, parents were instructed to coat their children's thumbs or fingers with a product called Stopzit®. They did this once in the morning when the children awoke, once just before bedtime, and once each time they observed an instance of thumb sucking, day or night. The results were impressive. The thumb-sucking habit of all seven children in the study rapidly declined to zero following the procedure.

Dental Appliances

In persistently stubborn cases, children's sucking habit can be broken with a dental device that's inserted into the mouth by a dentist. The metal appliance keeps the thumb from resting comfortably on the roof of the mouth. But the use of these devices to break sucking habits is controversial. Although many dentists report favorable results, others find the appliances ineffective and detrimental to a child's ability to eat and speak freely.

Talk with your dentist before you decide if this option is appropriate for your child. If all other techniques have failed and the sucking seems to be damaging social development and/or mouth and teeth formation, your dentist may be able to enlist your child's cooperation in trying the appliance as a final effort to break the habit.

Thumb and finger sucking is not a habit that's unavoidable or that must run its own course. You can effectively prevent the habit in infants, toddlers, and preschoolers. You can also intervene to stop it after the age of five without worrying about doing psychological damage by taking away a source of security. It's only when parents let the habit continue past this age that it is capable of inflicting physical and emotional damage.

Recommended for further reading for children:
David Decides
Susan M. Heitler, Ph.D.
Denver, Colo.: Reading Matters, 1985

5

Nail Biting

Nail biters may hide their fingertips in clenched fists or stand with their hands in their pockets, but there's no way to hide their habit forever. Eventually, in a handshake, or while passing the salt, or while signing their name, their fingertips become exposed and the unmistakable signs of nibbled edges and sore fingertips give them away. It's estimated that 40 million Americans are nail biters, making this habit a most common and persistent one. Unlike thumb sucking, which for the majority of affected children ceases before the end of the preschool years, nail biting follows the majority of those affected into adulthood. That's a strong reason for interrupting the habit in childhood before it becomes firmly entrenched.

The origins of the nail-biting habit can't always be pinpointed, but most often the practice can be traced to one of three sources. The habit may start as a substitute for proper nail maintenance; children who are bothered by long, rough, or broken nails will bite them to trim the edges. Some children become nail biters because they copy their parents or older siblings who bite their nails. And young children may bite their nails to release nervous energy. Regardless of its source, like many other bad habits, the habit stays long after the original cause disappears.

Habit Prevention

When you first notice your child nibbling at fingertips, you can begin a habit-prevention program to stop the behavior before it becomes an established habit.

Manicure
Prevent nail biting by filing down your child's nails. Very short nails are difficult to grab onto, and smooth rather than rough or jagged edges lessen the temptation to bite.

Praise
Nagging or scolding a young nail biter can lead to increased biting. So rather than even begin a power struggle that you'll eventually lose (no one can *make* children stop biting their own nails), approach the habit from the other direction—use praise. Catch your children when they're doing something constructive with their hands and comment that you're glad to see they're not biting their nails. Ignore them when they do bite.

Support
If your young children persist in their new nail-biting practice, explain your concern to family and friends. Tell grandparents, older siblings, and teachers that you want to stop the practice

before it becomes a habit, but you don't want to give it much attention. Encourage others to keep the child's hands busy, praise nonbiting moments, and ignore nibbling episodes.

Habit-Busting Strategies

When children are at least five years old, they're old enough to make a commitment to a habit-busting program. You'll need your children's cooperation to follow through to success, so it's most important that you begin the process with a persuasive discussion about the negative side of nail biting.

Nail biting is a habit with no redeeming qualities. It's not very soothing; it's generally not short-lived; it's self-injurious; and it's a source of constant social embarrassment. Help your children compare the "good" side ("I like to do it") with the bad side. Point out how nail biting can be painful when the nail is chewed down too far. Talk about how nibbled nails hurt the appearance of the hands and how many children grow up to be nail biters and become embarrassed on their jobs and with their friends because their nails look so stubby. Once your children agree to try to break their habit, you can begin the following habit-busting program.

Trigger Identification

Nail biting is often labeled a "nervous" habit. Sometimes stress does push young people to bite their nails as they seek an outlet for their nervous energy. But quite often even if the habit begins as a response to stress, the triggers that promote nail-biting episodes are everyday situations that can be controlled.

Use the monitoring chart on page 22 for one week before you begin the habit-busting process. Monitor your children's nail biting by adding an **X** mark every time you see them biting. Don't comment or interrupt them; just mark the time of day and note where they are and what they're doing. After one week of careful monitoring, you may see a pattern.

Seven-year-old Matthew's mom found that he bit his nails most ferociously during homework time every night. As soon as he opened his books, his left hand reached up to his mouth and he chewed continuously until the work was done. Matt also chewed while watching TV and riding in the car, but his homework nibbling was the most persistent.

If you find patterns of time or place in your child's nail-biting habit, ignore all but one biting circumstance and focus your habit-busting energies first on that one. Matt agreed to try to reduce his nail biting throughout the day, but the initial goal of his habit-busting program was the elimination of the nail biting during homework time.

Matt's mom explained to him that when his nail biting was substantially reduced during this time, he would then focus on TV time and then finally car time. By focusing little by little on the times and places Matt was most prone to nail biting, his habit would be gradually eliminated.

Self-Awareness

To help your children bring their habit from the subconscious level to a conscious one, set aside five minutes every morning and evening for mirror time. Instruct your children to watch themselves as they slowly bring their hand to their mouth and go through the motion of nail biting. (In the beginning, children may gain a truer picture of what they're doing by actually biting on their nails.) Nail biting is something you can't see yourself do, so this exercise gives children an idea of how they look to others and what they actually do with their mouth, arm, hand, fingers, and head. When they finish "nibbling," have your children say out loud, over and over, "I'm not going to do this anymore." Repeat this awareness tactic every morning and every night throughout the habit-busting program.

Additionally, awareness will grow each time you catch your children in the act. Without scolding or nagging, call attention to exactly what they're doing. Do they cup their fingers into their palm as they nibble? Do they rest their chin on the inside of their hand as they bite one nail at a time? Do they bite, tear, and pick at their nails or just bite? Add these findings to the mirror exercise each day.

Awareness can also be increased if you help your children notice other people's fingernails. Children need some perspective to understand why stubbly, chewed nails are unattractive. Comment when you see people with well-groomed hands. Use your own nails as an example; let your children join you each night as you clean, file, and care for your nails. Invite them to do the same to their own. Have your children look for examples of nice nails in magazines; then let them cut out these pictures and glue them on a piece of paper. This concentration on healthy, unbitten nails will give your children a clearer picture of what they're striving for.

Although Matt insisted that he did not bite his nails anymore, the condition of his nails told another story. Matt's mom helped him gain more awareness of his actions and their consequences by scheduling a nightly manicure session. She'd call Matt into her room to watch her care for her nails and cuticles. She talked out loud about what she was doing. She taught Matt how to clip, clean, and file nails. She asked him if he'd like to start taking care of his nails and then offered him his choice of manicure tools. Matt's habit wasn't beaten by awareness alone, but the tactic made him conscious of the appearance of his nails, which made him more willing to break the habit.

Response Prevention
Encourage your children to plan ways to prevent themselves from biting their nails before the urge strikes. Common prevention tactics include sitting on hands and keeping hands in pockets.

If these self-control methods don't keep the hand from straying to the mouth, your children might agree to try a more stringent preventive tactic. Some children wear mittens, gloves, or socks over their hands when they're in situations that spur nail biting. Children might, for example, place a pair of gloves next to the TV set and put them on before they sit down to watch a show if they know that TV viewing triggers nail biting.

Competing Response
If, despite preventive tactics, your children still get the urge to bite, they'll need to do something quickly with their hands that will compete with this urge. Your children might, for example, keep a nail file or emery board nearby for this kind of emergency. Instruct your children how to use them properly and then encourage them to file rather than bite their nails whenever the urge strikes.

Reduce nail-biting opportunities by keeping your children involved in hands-on activities. Idle hands often have a way of finding their way to a nibbler's mouth, so keep those hands busy. Offer puzzles, clay, crayons, or any toys that require hand manipulation.

When a nail file and toys aren't available or practical, teach your children to grab anything and hold on for at least one minute. Squeeze a pencil tightly; grab the edges of a book or the table; hold onto the arms of the chair; or make a tight fist. You might also give your children a small object that fits in their pocket that they can grab and hold when they feel the urge to bite. This object can be a small, smooth stone, a rabbit's foot, a string of beads, or anything that by its presence will remind them of their goal and will be there to help keep their hands away from their mouth.

If the monitoring chart (see page 22) shows that your children bite their nails as a nervous habit, dealing with the cause of the tension and practicing the relaxation exercises explained in Chapter 2 may save their nails. Matt's mother thought that perhaps tension had something to do with his nail biting during homework time. Matt's teacher had told her that although she had seen Matt bite his nails, he didn't do it continuously throughout the school day. So it seemed that working unsupervised at home made Matt nervous.

To combat the stress Matt felt at homework time, his mom changed his homework schedule to a time when she could sit down with him and guide him over his initial feelings of confusion and incompetence. Then Matt agreed to start the homework session with a short period of relaxation exercises. He would sit down and do a deep-breathing exercise (page 18) to calm his initial nervous reaction. Then he used positive thought control by saying out loud five times, "I can do this homework assignment and I can do a good job." Then with his mom nearby and his left hand squeezed tightly in a fist and placed on his lap, Matt began his homework.

Rewards and Penalties

Good intentions alone won't keep your children determined and motivated to break their nail-biting habit. The process can be long and frustrated by relapses, so when you first explain the habit-busting program, set up a reward-and-penalty system that will add some competitive fun to the venture. On the same chart you used to track down triggers, start a progress chart. Tell your children that each time you see them biting their nails during the restricted time period you'll put an X on their chart, and each time they resist biting for a fifteen-minute period you'll put a star or a happy face on the chart. Then construct a reward system as explained in Chapter 3 that allows your children to trade in their stars for a reward.

If your children do most of their biting during school hours, you'll need to alter the progress-chart technique. You might use a nail-examination technique to monitor progress. Every day as soon as the two of you meet after school, perform a nail examination in which you evaluate the condition of the nails. If they look untouched, put a star on the chart. If they appear chewed, put an X on the chart. Depending on your original agreement, stars may earn an immediate reward or they may be collected for a special prize at the end of the week.

The penalties for nail biting should be ones your children agree to as you're setting up your habit-busting program. You can't force children to stop nail biting with punishments like scoldings or spankings, but you can effectively use agreed-upon penalties. Ask your children what they think the penalty should be for nibbling during restricted times. If they're unsure or offer something inappropriate, you might suggest five minutes in a time-out chair, or reduced TV time, or an added chore like sweeping the kitchen floor. You might also plan a long-range penalty that would be imposed when the X marks on the progress chart add up to ten. The X's might mean cleaning the closet, or organizing the play area, or washing the dishes. Whatever the penalty, make sure your children agree in advance so the penalty is later imposed by their own actions—not you.

If your children seem to be fighting a losing battle, you can try more forceful penalties. Rubber-band therapy is a tactic that requires children to wear a quarter-inch-wide rubber band on their wrist. When they find themselves chewing their nails, they must pull the band back four to six inches and let go so it snaps the wrist. This may sound like a funny game to your children at first, but once they give it a try, they'll find out that it can serve as a strong reminder of their goal. As it hangs from the wrist, the rubber band itself serves as a reminder that helps children control their habit, but also the threat of self-inflicted pain encourages some children to reduce the number of times they bite each day.

Another penalty your children might want to try stops nail biting by providing an unpleasant reaction to the attempt. In any pharmacy you can buy a bitter-tasting liquid made specifically to be painted on children's fingertips. When they absentmindedly start to chew, the bitter taste makes them aware of what they're doing and interrupts the habit.

Rubber-band therapy and finger coating may sound like extreme tactics, but if your children are frustrated by repeated failures in the habit-busting program, they may agree to try these slightly harsh but often successful penalties.

Whatever rewards and penalties you use throughout the habit-busting process, don't forget the power of praise. Make sure you catch your child in a nonbiting moment every day and praise the effort.

Nail biting can be a tough habit to break. But because your children are young, their chances of leaving the habit behind are much better now than they will be later, when the act is firmly ingrained and their chewed fingertips cause constant social, career, and personal embarrassment. So if your children are ready to give it a try, build a program based on all the habit-busting strategies outlined in this chapter and stick to it. In about six to eight weeks, nail biting is likely to be a forgotten behavior of childhood.

Recommended for further reading for children:
The Berenstain Bears and the Bad Habit
Stan and Jan Berenstain
Random House, 1987

6

Hair Pulling

The embarrassment and shame associated with chronic hair pulling shrouds the habit in secrecy. Unlike nail biting and thumb sucking, which are openly discussed among parents, hair pulling is a hidden habit and often ignored when it first begins in early childhood in the hope that it will disappear. Unfortunately, children who continually give in to the urge to pull their own body hair may end up among the estimated 8 million Americans who suffer from trichotillomania. Trichotillomania is a long and technical term for the habit of pulling scalp, eyebrow, eyelash, beard, or mustache hairs. The unhealthy aspect of the habit doesn't become apparent until people notice that they have created a bald spot.

Some cases of trichotillomania are more than just habit and cannot be resolved with a self-help, habit-busting program. They stem from an obsessive-compulsive disorder, which is caused by a chemical imbalance in the brain. When this is the case, the symptoms usually begin with the hormonal changes of puberty.

The habit of hair pulling that appears in young children, however, is a learned response that is not rooted in a biochemical or psychological disorder. Like many bad habits, it begins in early childhood as a self-quieting or tension-release technique that continues after the original purpose is long forgotten. Eight-year-old Meg started pulling scalp hairs one at a time to unwind as she lay in bed at the end of each day. When I met Meg, she had been hair pulling for four years and was now wearing a hairpiece to hide the bald areas on the right side of her head. Her parents brought her to my clinic at Fairleigh Dickinson University after all their efforts to stop the habit had failed.

I was happy to assure Meg and her parents that there was nothing "wrong" with Meg. She most likely had no unresolved psychological problem. Nor was the habit a biochemical compulsion or a genetic quirk (although for unknown reasons, 90 percent of trichotillomanics are female). Like nail biters and thumb suckers, Meg had simply picked up a bad habit that could be eliminated.

Habit Prevention

After four years of hair pulling, Meg had established her habit so well that she and her family needed to jump right to habit-busting strategies. But if they had caught the practice when it first began, they could have used the following prevention strategies to stop hair pulling from becoming a habit.

Some children twirl a clump of hair around their finger and then pull; this weakens the roots and eventually hairs begin to fall out. Other children carefully select one strand and pull, then another and another, and so on until they've collected a pile of fallen hair. Whichever method your child uses, try not to give the practice too much attention when it first begins. When young children learn that they can get their parents' undivided attention by pulling on their hair, the frequency of hair pulling increases. Change your approach so you ignore hair pulling and praise nonhair-pulling moments. When you see your children watching TV without twirling or pulling hair, comment on how glad you are to see them sitting still without touching their hair. When your children catch on that they can get your attention and approval only when they're not pulling their hair, you'll see a decrease in the number of times each day they pull on their hair.

At the same time, change your child's hairstyle to make the habit more difficult to practice. Short hair on both boys and girls is more difficult to pull, especially if the pulling is preceded by twirling. Or, if your daughters have long hair that you don't want to cut, style it with barrettes, braids, a ponytail, or pigtails so it's more difficult to pull. If hair pulling has become a problem, don't let your children's hair hang long and loose. When they're consistently prevented from practicing the habit, most young children lose interest in the behavior.

If despite these preventive techniques you see your children pulling on their hair, distract them. Without scolding or calling attention to the habit, give your children something that will keep their hands busy. Give them a coloring book, molding clay, or a hands-on game. When the hands and mind are busy in play, they're not pulling hair. The less frequently your children pull their hair each day, the less likely the behavior will turn into a long-term habit.

Be sure to get preventive support from your children's

grandparents and care givers. Explain the problem and your decision not to call attention to it. Ask these people who spend time with your children to turn the children's attention to a hands-on activity when they notice hair pulling.

Habit-Busting Strategies

Most four- and five-year-olds are old enough to understand why hair pulling is harmful and to cooperate with a habit-busting program. Without showing annoyance or anger, explain to your children why you want them to stop pulling on their hair. Discuss the self-injurious, embarrassing, and messy aspects of the habit. Make them aware of the fact that hair pulling commonly leads to bald spots that will become permanent if the habit continues. If they laugh at the idea of going bald, bring them to the library. Look up trichotillomania in a medical encyclopedia; many of these books include a picture of a person's bald area. If your children, like Meg, are themselves balding, they already have reason enough to cooperate.

Trigger Identification

Before you implement habit-busting changes, take a week to watch your children and find out if their hair pulling is triggered by a specific time or place. Use the monitoring chart on page 22 to do this. Every time you see your children hair pulling, put an X in the appropriate space and write down what they were doing during the incident.

You may find that your children pull their hair most frequently when their hands are idle. This is often the case while watching TV, riding in the car, reading or, like Meg, when falling asleep.

Or you may find that your children reach for their hair when they feel tense. If hair pulling has become a nervous habit, the monitoring chart will probably show no specific time-of-day pattern, but you will see that the activity just before or during the hair pulling is a source of tension for your child. Homework, sports activities, sibling arguments, parental visitations, and the like can be very stressful for young children and can push them to find comfort and tension release in hair pulling.

Some researchers have suggested that for some youngsters, hair pulling is a way of releasing stored-up energy. If this is the case, your monitoring chart will show that hair-pulling episodes occur most frequently on days when your children have little opportunity to run around and be active.

It is also quite common for hair pullers to be thumb suckers. If thumb sucking triggers your children to reach for their hair, it's the thumb sucking that should be the focus of your habit-busting efforts. Use the program suggested in Chapter 4 to end thumb sucking and you'll see the hair-pulling habit resolve itself once its trigger is eliminated.

Self-Awareness
Once hair pulling becomes an ingrained habit, children will pull without any conscious awareness of their actions. Meg knew she pulled her hair while falling asleep because she had an ever-widening bald spot and a pillow full of hair every morning. But each morning she would swear to her parents that she didn't pull her hair the night before. Before habit-busting strategies can be effective, children need to bring their habit to a conscious level.

Mirror exercises are most helpful in helping children become aware of their habit. For three to five minutes every morning and every evening throughout the habit-busting process, have your children stand in front of a mirror while they pretend to pull hairs. Encourage them to describe out loud how they perform their habit. Which hand do they use? Do they twirl the strands first? Do they select one hair or grab several? Do they pull from the same spot all the time? Where do they put the hair that falls out? When you catch your children pulling during the day, point out the details of how they pull and add them to the mirror exercise that night.

To make your children aware of how much hair they pull out each day, instruct them to save the hairs that fall out and put them in a box. Together, examine the contents of the box at the end of the day and then have your children throw the hairs away. Don't ridicule or shame your children when you look at their collection. The goal is to make them aware of what they're doing. Knowing that what they pull will be saved and shown to you may encourage them to pull less hair the following day.

If your children have already pulled a bald spot, take a picture and hang it in a place where they can see it often. This constant reminder will increase their awareness and encourage them to end the habit. You can also use the picture as a visual point of comparison when the hair begins to grow back.

Response Prevention

If your children are having trouble breaking their habit, use response-prevention tactics to make it impossible for them to pull hairs. You can, for example, have them wear a hat during the time they most often pull. To get over the first, hardest hurdle of awareness and restraint, you can also use the nail biter's trick of splinting the inside of the elbow with tongue depressors and tape. This makes it impossible to bend the elbow and touch head or facial hairs. For instance, to prevent the habit, Meg's parents gave her gloves to wear to bed. Although the gloves made it difficult to pull hair, they didn't stop Meg. So then she put a thick sock over her hand and taped it to her arm. Finally, for the first time in four years, Meg made it through the night without pulling one hair from her head. She continued to wear the sock for ten nights until she felt the urge to pull had been weakened. At the same time, Meg used the following competing responses to resist her habit during the day.

Competing Response
The first thing Meg had to do was find a way to keep her hands occupied while she lay in bed. Children can do this by keeping a small ball, a rabbit's foot, or some similar small object always handy near their trigger situation — by the TV, or in the car, or with their homework materials, or, as in Meg's case, near the bed. Meg's parents gave her worry beads that she could manipulate between her fingers until she fell asleep.

You might also help your children practice keeping their hands busy when there's nothing to hold. They can, for example, sit on their hands, tap their fingers on the table, or clench their fists. Anything that keeps the hands busy and away from their hair will help reduce the number of hair-pulling episodes each day.

If your children pull hair as a response to stress, you can reduce the habit by teaching them other, more positive ways to handle tension. The relaxation exercises described in Chapter 2 are techniques that you should practice with your children over and over again. The idea is to replace the habit of responding to stress by hair pulling with the habit of deep breathing or positive imagery. Once they've learned the techniques, constantly remind them to relax *before* they enter the stressful situation. If they do this consistently, soon a healthy tension-relief habit will replace the old.

Rewards and Penalties

Meg was delighted the first night her monitoring chart showed no hair-pulling incidents. She was proud of her success, but she was also happy because she earned the reward promised by her mother—a trip to the beauty parlor. Meg wanted to stop pulling her hair for health reasons, but like all children she needed more incentive to keep trying. A reward-and-penalty system will motivate your children to keep working at the habit-busting process after the initial burst of enthusiasm passes.

As you begin your program, explain to your children that when they remember to keep their hands away from their hair, they can earn rewards like small toys or special privileges like Meg's. But also warn them that when they do pull their hair they must pay a penalty such as five minutes in a time-out chair or a reduction in TV time or playtime.

Use the monitoring chart on page 22 as a progress chart. You can mark nonpulling periods during the daily situations that usually trigger pulling by putting stars or happy faces in the appropriate spaces. These stars can be traded in for a prize or they can be saved and turned in at the end of the week for a special privilege. Talk with your children and together decide which rewards to offer. In the beginning when the habit is still strong, you may need to offer small rewards every time you catch your children making an effort to practice a competing response. As the habit weakens, you can stretch out the time required to earn a reward.

At the same time, use the progress chart to mark hair-pulling episodes. Every time you see your children pulling their hair in the trigger situation, put an X in the appropriate space and impose an agreed-upon penalty. If, for example, Meg's mom checked on her at bedtime and found her hand touching her hair, she put an X on her chart and reminded Meg that she had lost ten minutes of TV time in the morning. If Meg's mom caught her touching her hair again fifteen minutes later, she added another X and decreased TV time by another ten minutes.

Rewards and penalties should focus only on the triggers you uncover with the monitoring chart. It's too hard to begin a habit-busting program with the promise "never" to pull hair again. But agreeing to stop during one particular time of the day is a manageable quest that gives your children a feeling of control without being overwhelmed. If you find your children pulling their hair at other times of the day, call their attention to it and ask them to stop, but don't impose penalties. When that trigger situation is under control, move on to another time of day, and so on until slowly the habit is broken.

Social rewards, like praise, approval, and encouragement, can and should be used throughout the day. Praise your children often when you catch them in nonhair-pulling situations. Compliment their efforts as often as possible. Comment on their willpower and determination. Repeatedly let them know that you're happy they've decided to do something positive about their bad habit.

7

Stuttering

The Speech Foundation of American estimates that 25 percent of all children go through a period of stuttering (called disfluency) between the ages of two and six. That's why two-and-a-half-year-old Tommy's pediatrician wasn't concerned when his mom brought him in for a speech evaluation. Tommy spoke quite well for his age but sometimes (typically when excited or worried) he'd repeat initial sounds like this: "I wa...wa...wa ...wa...want to go ou...ou...ou...outside."

The pediatrician assured Tommy's mother that at this age, Tommy's speech pattern was not a cause for alarm. He gave her a list of dos and don'ts similar to the ones offered later in this chapter that can keep a speech disfluency from becoming a long-term habit. He also emphasized that stuttering is not a symptom of emotional or psychological disturbance. As *American Health* magazine recently reported, more than 2.6 million Americans stutter, and as cases are examined it's found repeatedly that the distress of stuttering may cause emotional and psychological problems, not the other way around.°

Why Kids Stutter

As young children begin to stutter, all parents want to know why. The answer is not always easy to pinpoint. A few theories that are most widely accepted by the professional community are explained below. In most cases, children stutter due to a combination of these factors.

Speech is a complex process involving the brain, respiratory and nervous systems, and one hundred different muscles. Each must work in coordination to produce even the most basic speech sound. Sometimes, as children practice linguistic skills, one of these speech components falters. Often children's motor abilities lag behind their mental development, so although they may have a mental image of what they want to say, they have difficulty finding and pronouncing the right words and phrases to express themselves quickly—and so they stutter.

Some speech pathologists believe that children stutter because the brain does not function normally when they try to organize thoughts and translate them into speech. Faulty transmission of nerve impulses within the brain, for example, or between the brain and the various muscles and mechanisms used in speech, may be the cause. It may also be that one side of the brain is sending and receiving signals faster than the other, causing confusion to the speakers who do not accurately

°Judith Fertig, "A New Technique to Stop Stuttering," *American Health,* October 1991, p. 89.

hear the sounds they produce. And some experts think that the problem is a malfunction in the auditory mechanism that creates a slight lag between the time speakers produce a sound and the time they hear it.

Some children's stutter may be a physical reaction to tension. We all react physically to stress: Sometimes our neck muscles tense, or our abdomen tightens, or our hands clench. Some people experience a muscle spasm of the larnyx and vocal cords that blocks the smooth flow of sound and causes stuttering.

There also seems to be a genetic predisposition to stuttering. Children of stutterers are more likely than other children to stutter, even when the parent stopped stuttering long before the child was born. But it's not clear if the problem is biologically inherited or if the parent's emotional reaction to the stutter causes it to worsen and continue. It is also a well-known but little-understood fact that boys are five times more likely to stutter than girls.

There is no *one* accepted theory to explain stuttering because for each explanation there's an exception. If the problem is neurological, why can stutterers sing and yell without stuttering? If the problem is a physical reaction to stress, why do stutterers handle some very stressful situations without stuttering? If the problem is genetic, why do some stutterers have no family history of the problem? There are many unanswered questions in the search for the cause of stuttering. There is, however, one fact about stuttering that is absolute: Stuttering that starts as a perfectly normal, developmental behavior can become a lifelong habit if it is handled incorrectly in its early stages.

Habit Prevention

How you react to the first signs of disfluent speech will set the stage for how your children will manage the problem. The more often negative attention is drawn to the stuttering, the more likely it is to increase in frequency and severity. This happens when the children become frustrated and the tension turns into fear of speaking. They may learn to avoid certain words and shy away from speaking situations. Their stuttering, which may have begun merely in response to their desire to speak quickly, can soon worsen when combined with anticipatory stress—a fear of what will happen if they try to speak. That stress alone can keep them stuttering years after the fear that started it has long passed.

The following early management strategies are most appropriate for stutterers between two and five years old. They can help prevent the anxious feelings that affect a young stutterer's ability to communicate with social and emotional security. If your child is over five, the following suggestions will certainly ease the problem, but they need to be combined with professional therapy as explained later in the chapter.

What To Do About Stuttering

1. Ignore stuttering in the early stages. Young children show no awareness of their disfluency. If you don't call attention to it when it begins, the child has a much better chance of outgrowing it.

2. Slow down everything. A slow-paced household gives children more opportunity to talk without stress. It allows time for

everyone to be heard without having to compete with each other for a few seconds of attention. Harried schedules make children feel they must speak quickly and rush their thoughts into words; this sense of urgency fosters stuttering.

3. Model relaxed speech patterns. Speak slowly and use short sentences. Pause occasionally between sentences and use simple vocabulary appropriate to your child's age. Show your children through your own example that language doesn't need to be rushed or complex.

4. Listen when your children talk. Whenever possible, look at them and give them your full attention; this will eliminate body language that says, "I'm busy; hurry up and say what you have to say." Listen patiently to the whole story; this communicates that you're interested in the content of what your children have to say, not the way it is said.

What *Not* To Do About Stuttering

1. Don't tell your children how to stop stuttering. Telling young children who stutter to slow down, take a deep breath, or think about what they have to say before they speak is advice that won't solve the problem, and it suggests that children are at fault for speaking the wrong way.

2. Don't cut them off. Let your children stutter through their sentences without help, correction, or interruption. When you call attention to a stutter, it is likely to increase in severity and frequency.

3. Don't get upset. Just as you let your children stumble without reprimand or anxiety when they learned to walk, let them stumble as they learn to talk. Never yell, scold, or say, "Stop it!" Also, watch your body language; if you won't look in your child's eyes, or constantly look away, or pick up busywork when your child stutters, you're conveying distress.

4. Don't expect consistency. Children may go through long periods of perfect fluency and then unexpectedly revert to stuttering again. Stuttering may stop and start for several years. The fact that children can speak smoothly sometimes doesn't mean they have complete control of the problem and are being lazy or obstinate when it reappears. Inconsistency is a standard characteristic of early disfluency.

5. Don't push your child to speak. Try to avoid situations in which your child will be asked to "tell Aunt Gloria what happened today." Children who are continually embarrassed by their speech may soon stop talking altogether.

Beyond a Normal Stutter

When Tommy's mother left her pediatrician's, she read over a list of preventive strategies similar to the one above and incorporated many of the suggestions into her daily routine. Still, over the following year the stutter became more frequent and more pronounced. So again she brought Tommy to the pediatrician. Now that Tommy was almost four years old, the doctor thought perhaps he should see a speech pathologist. But before making that recommendation, he and Tommy's mother discussed the following criteria, which help parents distinguish between normal developmental disfluency and speech patterns that put a child at risk for ongoing speech problems.

COMMON DISFLUENCY	AT-RISK DISFLUENCY
1. Repeats whole words: "I saw, I saw, I saw a dog."	1. Repeats initial sound or part of a word: "I s-s-s-saw a dog."
2. Pauses filled with um, ah, uh: "I saw um, um, um, a dog."	2. Holds an empty pause for more than a second: "I s— aw a dog."
3. Single repetition of initial sound: "I s-saw a dog."	3. The first sound is not repeated but held and drawn out: "I sssssaw a dog."

Children experiencing common disfluency usually appear unaware of the stuttering and show no apparent stress. When they begin to react to the speech problem (usually because those around them do), the core of stuttering as a continuing habit is formed. The Speech Foundation of America offers these six symptoms that indicate when the situation is becoming serious and should be brought to the attention of a speech pathologist:

1. Trembling in the muscles around the mouth and jaw.

2. A rise in pitch and loudness during the stutter.

3. Struggle and tension in speech.

4. Coping mechanisms such as rolling eyes, blinking, and head jerks.

5. Fear and unhappiness about having to speak.

6. Avoidance of a particular word or of speech altogether.

Tommy's mother had noticed several of these symptoms in his speech pattern. In the past month, he had begun to close his eyes and tap his foot on the floor when he struggled to get past a stutter. He cried when his mother forced him to bring a show-and-tell item to his preschool class. And he would often start to tell her a story but then stop short and run to his room when he thought he might stutter. Tommy had begun to fear his stutter and so it became worse and was now showing signs of habit. His mother and the doctor agreed it was time to have Tommy's speech evaluated by a specialist.

Habit-Busting Strategies

If your children are of school age and have any of the six symptoms listed above, you should have the problem evaluated by a professional speech pathologist. When children begin pre-scribed therapy at this age, the results are most often quite successful. For a referral to a speech pathologist, ask your pediatrician, call your local university or medical center, or contact the Speech Foundation or the American Speech-Language-Hearing Association, listed at the end of this chapter.

Although the strategies commonly used to stop stuttering are similar to those recommended throughout this book, I strongly suggest that you don't try to self-treat this problem.

The complex interweaving of physical and emotional factors that cause stuttering in older children requires professional treatment, which may include the following:

Shaping: A speech therapist may use a technique called fluency shaping, which seeks to modify the entire speech pattern. Stutterers start by pronouncing words very slowly and then gradually increasing speed.

Trigger Monitoring: Because stuttering can be sparked by a stressful situation and may be aggravated by specific words, monitoring charts like the one on page 22 are often used to identify a child's stutter triggers.

Awareness Exercises: Some therapists use a mirror exercise to foster awareness of what happens during a stuttering episode. Children are encouraged to watch themselves in a mirror as they speak. They look for muscular tension, breathing difficulties, and any quirky body movements.

Competing Response: The frequency of stuttering can often be decreased if the child learns relaxation exercises like those described in Chapter 2. These are especially helpful if the problem is exaggerated by stress.

Response Prevention: Techniques that prevent the stutter from occurring are often the focus of speech-therapy sessions. Children can learn to intercept the physical responses that cause the stutter and then produce fluent speech. Techniques include breathing exercises that teach a stutterer to exhale before each sentence to reduce the tension in the vocal cords, and to inhale fully at short but appropriate intervals to create deliberate pauses in the speech pattern.

A therapist will use a combination of these techniques along with others that emphasize regularized and relaxed breathing patterns, oral reading exercises, word stress and pause changes, and most certainly opportunities to improve self-image and attitude.

For more information about stuttering, call:

▶ Speech Foundation of America (800) 992–9392
In Washington, D.C., call (202) 363–3199

▶ American Speech-Language-Hearing Association
(800) 638–8255
In Maryland, call (301) 897–8682

Recommended for further reading for children:
Lost Boys Never Say Die
Alan Brown and Grant Forsberg
Delacorte Press, 1989

Recommended for further reading for parents:
Stutter No More
Martin F. Schwartz
Simon & Schuster, 1991

8

Teeth Grinding

When children continually grit and grind their teeth, the habit is known as bruxism. This habit, which affects about 14 percent of children ages three to seventeen, is more than just annoying; it can seriously affect the child's teeth and jaws and cause facial soreness and headaches. It can also lead to temporomandibular (TMJ) disorders, which affect the joints that connect the lower jaw to the skull. This problem plagues an estimated 10 million Americans, who experience earaches, muscle spasms, and excruciating pain through the head and neck. If your children are in the habit of grinding their teeth, you should not wait for them to outgrow it. They probably will not, and the consequences of dental and facial malformations as well as possible long-term health problems make bruxism a habit to be dealt with early.

There have been many theories about the causes of bruxism that are no longer supported by the medical community.

Unfortunately, the beliefs persist and cause many parents to worry unnecessarily. Rest assured that bruxism is not a symptom of emotional illness or the expression of anger, anxiety, hate, or aggression. It is not a sign of a neurological disorder that necessarily precedes epilepsy, cerebral palsy, or Down's syndrome. It has also recently been determined that bruxism is not caused by dental problems such as an incorrect bite or uneven edges. John Dodes, D.D.S., of The National Council Against Health Fraud, cautions us to avoid dentists who treat bruxism by changing the shape of the teeth. "To grind your teeth down or build them up," he says, "will not stop bruxism. That is quackery."°

The dental community isn't sure exactly what does cause children to grind, grit, and clench their teeth. The most widely held belief looks to a genetic predisposition that is aggravated by stress. Stress tends to make children tense their facial muscles and tighten their jaws. The stress may promote grinding and then continue on as a habit even after the tension is gone. Grinding is most commonly practiced during sleep, and these nocturnal gnashers are also likely to clench their teeth during the day.

Habit Prevention

Many infants grind their new teeth. This helps file down the sharp points and it appears to ease the discomfort of teething. This grinding action is not considered an early sign of bruxism. If, however, bruxism runs in your family, you might encourage your infant to find other ways to ease the discomfort of teething.

°Stephanie Ebbert, "Your Health Smile," *Prevention*, August 1991, p. 90.

Offer plastic teething rings and textured foods like zwieback, apple slices, or small bits of cheese. If the practice persists past the teething period, you can then begin to reduce the likelihood of bruxism in a toddler by practicing the habit-busting strategies of awakening and the adjustment of sleep position that don't require full cooperation from a young child. Once children are over the age of three, they can understand the danger their habit can cause to their teeth, gums, and muscles of the mouth and jaw, and they can cooperate with the following habit-busting strategies.

Trigger Identification

Ten-year-old Anne was in the habit of grinding her teeth while she slept. The habit didn't bother Anne, it didn't disturb her sleep, and she seemed to have no awareness of the problem. Her parents, however, could no longer stand the grinding sound that had been keeping them awake for years, and they were worried that the habit might damage her teeth.

Sleep seemed to be the obvious trigger that activated Anne's grinding episodes. But still I asked Anne's parents, Joyce and Nathan, to monitor the nighttime habit closely for two weeks. They were instructed to write down the date and the exact time they heard the grinding. And using the monitoring chart on page 22, they were also asked to record daytime occurrences of teeth or jaw clenching. After two weeks Joyce and Nathan were surprised to find that there was definitely a pattern to Anne's grinding episodes.

Anne didn't grind her teeth every night. The written record showed that there was a relationship between nighttime grinding and daytime clenching. For example, Anne's grinding woke her parents on the second night of record keeping; her daytime monitoring chart showed that during that previous day Anne had clenched her teeth as she struggled to repair a broken toy, as she tried to complete a difficult homework assignment, and during the entire time her dad scolded her about leaving her bike in the street. This daytime clenching and nighttime grinding pattern repeated itself eight times over the recorded two-week period. Anne's parents could now easily see that the real trigger was not sleep; it was daytime stress.

If your children grind their teeth at night, keep track of their daytime levels of tension. Be sure to keep written records so you don't overlook a pattern or forget occurrences. If you find no pattern of day/stress relationship, there may be other, as yet undiscovered reasons for your child's habit. Or it may be that the grinding behavior is so ingrained that it now exists without its original stress trigger.

Self-Awareness
Because most teeth grinding is practiced while children are asleep, and most teeth clenching is a nervous response they can't see, you'll need to help your children become more aware of their habit. Explain the health dangers associated with teeth grinding and then lead your children to a mirror. Tell them to clench their back teeth and watch how their facial appearance changes. Instruct them to relax their jaw and breathe through their mouth. Call your children's attention to how the feel and look of the face changes. Ask them to describe how their jaw feels when it's tensed and how it feels when it's relaxed. Let your children practice tightening and relaxing the jaw in front of the mirror every day for about two minutes throughout the habit-busting program. This exercise helps them become more aware of the habit that needs their conscious effort to break.

Competing Response

The following habit-busting techniques have all been success-fully used to break the teeth-grinding habit. You may have to experiment with each until you find the tactic or combination of tactics that gives your child relief.

Relaxation: The following techniques can reduce nighttime grinding for two reasons: (1) When practiced immediately be-fore bedtime, they reduce the jaw tension that builds up during the day and often seeks relief in nocturnal grinding. (2) When practiced in the daytime, they retrain the body's stress response and again reduce jaw tension.

Open-Mouth Breathing: Similar to the deep-breathing exercise de-scribed in Chapter 2, open-mouth breathing is a technique that can retrain a person's stress response by interrupting body tension and taking in extra oxygen (it also keeps the jaw from tensing). Teach your child to face stressful situations (like teacher scoldings, athletic competitions, and public speaking assignments) by breathing slowly and deeply for about three minutes through a slightly opened mouth. Remind your children of this exercise every time you see them begin to clench. When you see them practice the technique in a stressful situation without being reminded, you'll know the grinding habit is al-most broken.

Guided Imagery: Similar to the above technique, guided imagery can retrain a person's daily stress response, and this in turn can reduce the jaw tension that often leads to nighttime grinding. The details of this technique are outlined in Chapter 2.

Muscle Relaxation: This technique is quite simple and yet has proven highly effective in many cases. Instruct your children to do the following:

▶ Clench their teeth firmly for about five seconds.

▶ Relax for five seconds.

▶ Repeat four to six times a day.

Studies have found that as many as 75 percent of bruxists stopped grinding their teeth after twenty-one days of this self-treatment. The key is consistency. Make sure your children don't skip their exercise periods.

Adjustment of Sleep Position

Bruxism can be caused by the sleep position. Children who sleep on their side may put pressure on the nerves of the face that prompt grinding. If your children grind only while sleeping on their side, encourage them to sleep on their back. It usually takes three to four nights to adapt to a change of position, so you can help ease the adjustment by propping pillows alongside the child's body to inhibit rolling. If in their sleep your children roll back to their side, return them to their back.

Some children simply cannot sleep on their back. When this is the case, you can ease the pressure on the side of the face by giving your children a soft head pillow and placing another pillow under their upper arm.

Awakening

Some studies have observed that bruxism takes place primarily during the fourth sleep stage of rapid eye movement (REM).

Although there is no documented connection between dreams and grinding, some clinicians have helped teeth grinders reduce the frequency of their habit by repeatedly awakening them at the first signs of clenching or grinding. This method will require diligent attention on your part, but the results after even one week may be significant enough to encourage you to continue until the habit is completely broken.

The moment you hear your children begin to grind, wake them up and have them relax their jaw completely or reposition them so they're on their back. Continue this procedure throughout the night every night for two weeks to see if it has a positive effect.

Response Prevention

In severe cases of bruxism, a dentist may prescribe a custom-fitted bite guard to prevent further injury to the teeth. If your children suffer aching jaws, headaches on one side, or a misaligned jawbone, and they do not show signs of reduced grinding after using the above habit-busting techniques for one month, ask your dentist to check for chipped and worn teeth. The dentist may decide to put a plastic plate or splint over the upper or lower teeth to prevent further damage. This approach will not permanently stop the habit, however. Although some families have found that the bite guard reduces the number and severity of grinding episodes, these positive effects last only as long as the guard is used. So even with a bite guard in place, your child will still benefit from a habit-busting program.

Rewards and Penalties

Children need motivation to continue their efforts to break a bad habit. Bruxism, however, poses a dilemma when trying to establish a reward-and-penalty system because most often the habit is practiced while the child is sound asleep and completely unaware of success or failure. For this reason, an incentive program is best focused on your child's willingness to cooperate and practice the habit-busting strategies, rather than the mastery of the grinding habit itself.

You might, for example, use the monitoring chart to keep track of your children's relaxation exercise periods. Every time they practice a technique, they earn a star on the chart. Every time they remember to use these techniques without being reminded, give them two stars. Then, when they earn a specified number, let them cash in their stars for a special treat or privilege.

Penalties can be imposed in much the same way. Tell your children in advance that if they don't practice their habit-busting techniques, then their TV watching or video playing time will be reduced that day. If they grind while watching TV, turn the set off for three minutes. These negative consequences will remind them to cooperate and pay attention to their habit in the future.

Don't forget social rewards. Praise, encouragement, and approval are always effective in motivating children to kick a habit. Every day during the habit-busting period, remind your children of your certainty that they can end the habit. And comment positively on *any* effort they make to reduce the frequency of daytime clenching or grinding.

Because Anne's grinding habit was so obviously related to stress, her parents chose to begin their program with self-awareness and relaxation exercises. After a day of discussion and practice, Anne and her family set up this schedule: As part of her morning wash-up routine, Anne stood in front of the mirror and watched herself perform the muscle-relaxation exercise. Then, during her ride to school, she practiced open-mouth breathing. On the ride home from school, she again used open-mouth breathing, and before she changed into her play clothes, she again washed up and practiced her muscle-relaxation exercises in front of the mirror. Finally, when Anne got into bed each night, she practiced both open-mouth breathing and muscle relaxation.

Just before sleep, Anne updated her progress chart. For every time she remembered to practice her relaxation exercises that day, she earned a star. Every time she remembered to use the techniques without being reminded, she earned two stars. And anytime she used a relaxation response rather than clenched teeth in a stressful situation, she earned five stars. When Anne earned twenty stars, she was promised a video movie party with her best friend.

Three weeks after she started the program, Joyce and Nathan noted a slight yet steady decrease in Anne's nighttime grinding. Six months later, they reported that the grinding habit had almost disappeared. They still encouraged Anne to avoid daytime clenching, and on the infrequent occasions when they heard her grinding at night, they would wake her up to do relaxation exercises. "As far as I'm concerned, the problem is resolved," wrote her dad. "There are occasional relapses, but we know how to handle them and they are so infrequent we're no longer worried about the damage grinding might do to Anne's teeth."

Within one month after starting a habit-busting program that includes trigger identification, self-awareness, response-prevention strategies, and a system of rewards and penalties, you too should see marked improvement in your children's teeth-grinding habit. If you do not, don't consider the habit unconquerable. Because of the serious long-term health effects of this habit, ask your dentist or pediatrician to recommend another course of action. Some families find it helpful to have professional guidance through a program similar to the one explained in this chapter. Others have been successfully guided out of this habit through hypnosis, and most recently many have been able to eliminate the problem completely through professionally administered biofeedback.

Masturbation and Self-Touching

Childhood masturbation and self-touching are universal activities and normal aspects of self-exploration for both boys and girls. By eighteen months of age, all children have discovered their genitals and many masturbate. You should not, however, associate this action with the sexual behavior and feelings experienced by adults. Children masturbate and fondle their genitals for two primary reasons: (1) because they are learning that their sex organs are a source of sensual (not sexual) pleasure; and/or (2) because, like thumb sucking, the act gives comfort and relieves tension.

You should not try to break the habit of masturbation or self-touching because you think it's abnormal or harmful. It should be broken because it has become a *habit*—a learned behavior that's repeated so often it has become automatic and persistent—and because it's often performed in public where self-stimulation is not a socially acceptable behavior. If your children masturbate occasionally in your home, ignore it. But if they masturbate or fondle themselves excessively and/or in public, then they need your help to break the habit.

Because there's nothing fundamentally wrong with masturbation or self-touching, the approach to stopping these behaviors is a bit different from the strategies used to end harmful habits such as hair pulling or nail biting. You will not want to associate the practice with words like *bad* or *harmful*. A negative attitude can pass on feelings of guilt, shame, embarrassment, or anxiety that can later affect a child's adult view of self and sexuality. The following habit-busting program focuses solely on the *habit* aspect of masturbating and self-touching, not the behaviors themselves.

Habit Prevention

Although the acts of masturbation and self-touching are natural, you can keep these actions from becoming habit by reducing the number of times the behavior is practiced. When you see your children masturbating or find your little boys holding their penises, don't overreact. Don't scold; don't call attention to the act; don't abruptly change their position. Instead, calmly transfer their attention away from their body to some other activity. Quite matter-of-factly, invite them to play a game of checkers, or color a picture, or squeeze some clay. If they resist your invitation, gently distract their attention by physically guiding them toward something else. Make no comment about what they were doing. The goal of prevention is simply to reduce the time spent masturbating or self-touching.

Trigger Identification

Knowing when and where your children most often masturbate will help you break the habit. You should use the monitoring chart on page 22 to keep track of patterns, but don't make your monitoring efforts too obvious. At this stage in the habit-busting program, your children will not understand the difference between the normal acts of masturbating and self-exploration and the negative aspects of such a habit. Obvious monitoring can cause confusion and embarrassment.

After one week of monitoring, look for a predictable pattern. If you find that your children masturbate or self-touch most often when they're tense, the relaxation approach explained below will be most effective. If you find that boredom triggers the problem, the following response-prevention tactics will be most helpful. If you see a trigger in an activity like TV watching, you can reduce the habit by limiting the amount of time spent in the trigger activity. But if you find that your child masturbates anywhere and anytime without a particular pattern, you'll best control the habit by focusing first on one time or place.

Three-year-old Max, for example, would lie on the floor and masturbate at moments his mother, Diane, could never have predicted or prevented. During one week of monitoring, Diane recorded thirty episodes of masturbation. She realized she could not possibly interrupt every occurrence without losing her patience and calling negative attention to the habit, so she decided to concentrate first on masturbation episodes outside the home. You too might want to limit your initial focus to one trigger, and when that circumstance is under control, then move to another.

Self-Awareness

Because it's a habit, your children may have no awareness of when, where, or how often they masturbate. The usual technique of mirror practice is certainly not appropriate for this habit because it might embarrass your child and would detract from the message of privacy you want to convey. But still, you need to help your children become more aware of what they're doing.

Approach your children in the act at a moment when the two of you are alone in the house and explain in an understanding way what you want them to do in the future. You might say something like, "I know you like to rub yourself in this way, but this is something people do when they're alone, not in front of others. So from now on, why don't you do it only when you're alone in your room." End your discussion with a hug and a smile.

Another awareness technique relies on prompting. Children who masturbate may need their habit interrupted by their parents many times before they become fully aware of what they're doing. However, you won't want to interrupt the act by yelling, "Hey, you're masturbating again." Tell your children that you will help them remember the agreement to keep masturbation in the bedroom by using a special, secret signal as a reminder. Diane told Max she would call his name when she noticed him masturbating and she would wink to remind him of their deal. If your children don't respond to their name, you may need to touch their shoulder before giving the secret signal. Remember, whatever method you use, avoid any reminders that are loud, angry, or embarrassing.

Response Prevention

Response prevention incorporates strategies that make it impossible to practice a given habit. An elbow splint keeps a nail biter's fingers away from the face; mittens keep a thumb sucker's thumb out of the mouth. But because children find innumerable ways and places and positions in which to masturbate, you'll need to consider carefully their individual style to discover methods of prevention.

Diane knew that Max always masturbated lying on his stomach. In this case, response prevention was possible by keeping Max in a sitting position. As soon as Diane saw Max lie down (which he would often do in the car and while waiting on line in stores or at the bank), she would scoop him up, remind him of their agreement, and prevent the habit from occurring.

Competing Response

A competing response helps children break a habit by giving them something else to do instead of the undesirable behavior. In the case of masturbation, you can help your children ease tension that may be causing their behavior by substituting relaxation exercises for masturbation. The three relaxation exercises explained in Chapter 2 are all appropriate competing responses for masturbation. Diane chose to teach Max deep breathing because she felt it would be the easiest to teach to a three-year-old. They practiced the exercise at home each night before Max went to bed, and then Diane and Max agreed that every time she called his name and winked to interrupt his habit during the day, he would stop and practice one minute of deep breathing.

If you know where and when your children are most likely to masturbate, you can reduce the likelihood of the behavior if you provide other activities in those circumstances. Diane knew that Max was bound to masturbate in the car and when waiting on line in stores, so she put small games, books, and puzzles in the backseat of the car to give him something else to do. She also loaded her pocketbook with snacks, trinkets, and snapshots that she knew would keep Max occupied when he became bored while shopping. These competing responses reduced the likelihood of Max masturbating in public.

If your little boy is in the habit of holding his penis, you can weaken the habit by keeping his hands busy. Ask him to hold your bags at the store. Give him a ball to squeeze or your spare keys to jingle as you say good-bye to your in-laws. Give him a rabbit's foot or a tennis ball to carry for "good luck" whenever you go out in public. When you use your secret code to draw his attention to the habit, teach him to let go of his penis and then tighten his fingers into a fist and hold for several seconds and then relax. Tell him to repeat this exercise several times.

Rewards and Penalties

If the habit is persistent and excessive and your children cannot remember to refrain from public masturbation, you can help them by offering a positive incentive. Before you go to your boss's barbecue, for instance, remind your children of the agreement not to rub themselves in public; then offer a specific reward for remembering this promise. The reward should be something you can give immediately after the visit, or it may even be several small items you can give every hour throughout the day.

Max's mom bought a five-pack box of soft clay. She told Max that she would give him one color each time they returned home from a public place where he did not rub himself. On the first day, Diane and Max left the house on three occasions, and at the end of the day Max had two containers of clay. On one trip Max masturbated in the back of the car, so Diane calmly kept her promise and did not give him clay when they returned home. Although Max cried and pleaded, Diane remained firm; when they went to visit Max's grandmother the next day, Max had no trouble remembering his agreement and he earned another box of clay.

For varied psychological and emotional reasons, it's not a good idea to punish children for seeking sensual pleasure. It's almost impossible to impose a penalty to break the habit of masturbating without making the child feel that the penalty is related to the act of self-stimulation itself. The withholding of a promised reward for noncompliance is penalty enough in this situation.

Childhood masturbation and self-touching are certainly more embarrassing for the parents than for the children involved. Keep this in mind as you try to break the habit. Your children are innocently following natural urges. Don't give in to the temptation to shout, "Will you stop that!" "Stopping" is not the goal of this habit-busting program. Rather, you want to direct these behaviors into a more acceptable environment and convey to your children the private nature of self-stimulation.

Recommended for further reading for parents:
Growing Up, Feeling Good: A Child's Introduction to Sexuality
Stephanie Waxman
Panjandrum, 1979

10

Tics

A tic is a sudden, nonpurposeful muscle spasm. The tic habit can show itself in behaviors such as shrugging, blinking, squinting, shoulder or head jerking, grimacing, head shaking or nodding, or nose wrinkling. These motor tics are fairly common in childhood; in fact, the American Psychiatric Association has documented that 5 to 24 percent of children have a history of some kind of tic.° It's also been found that tics affect males three times more often than females and that chronic tics are most frequently observed between the ages of six and twelve.

Transient Tics

Common motor tics often begin at about three and a half years of age. They help children release nervous energy, and 75 per-

°*Diagnostic and Statistical Manual of Mental Disorders* (Washington, D.C.: American Psychiatric Association, 1987), p. 82.

cent of the children outgrow the tic within six months.* If your young child begins a tic behavior, it's best to simply ignore it. Don't call attention to it or nag your child to stop. You might help prevent the action from becoming a habit by practicing the prevention strategies explained later in this chapter, but transient tics should not be addressed with the full habit-busting program.

Chronic Tics

If a tic continues for more than twelve months, it's considered a chronic tic. Chronic tics are persistent and the muscle spasm is usually quite exaggerated. They typically occur in bouts and their intensity often changes from month to month, from day to day, or even from one hour to the next. In fact, the tic behavior may completely disappear for weeks or months at a time and then reappear. Chronic tics can and should be stopped with the program explained in this chapter.

Causes

It was once believed that tics were an outward sign of repressed feelings and conflicts. Today they are widely viewed as a combination of biological and environmental factors. A family history of tics is found in approximately one-third of all cases, which leads many researchers to believe that the problem may have a genetic basis, or in some cases it may also mean that the habit can be picked up through imitation. It's also known that

*Pam Miller, "Creatures of Habit," *Child*, June/July 1991, p. 118.

tic behaviors increase in times of stress, giving rise to the label "nervous tic."

Caution

It is not appropriate to use this habit-busting program to treat tics that are caused by a psychoneurotic disorder called Tourette's syndrome. Like chronic tics, Tourette's syndrome can begin with a single tic of the eye, face, or head, which appears between the ages of two and fifteen, typically around age seven or eight. Quite different from chronic tics, however, Tourette's syndrome often affects multiple muscle groups and causes involuntary behaviors such as sniffling, hacking, throat clearing, tongue protrusion, snorting, barking, or other uncommon noises. It also can prompt impulsive outbursts of shouting or swearing. The presence of motor tics plus noise-making in a child who exhibits hyperactive and self-destructive behaviors strongly suggests Tourette's syndrome and indicates the problem is not safely or appropriately treated as a bad habit.

If your child suffers a chronic muscular tic that is not accompanied by persistent, involuntary vocal noises, the following habit-busting program can be successfully used. If the tic has been present for more than a year and is persistent and exaggerated, it's best to break the habit now.

Habit Prevention

If your family has a history of tic behaviors, there are several ways you can reduce the likelihood of chronic tic development in your child. If your child already suffers from tics, the following information can be used to reduce the frequency and intensity of their occurrence.

Reduce Stress: Because tic behaviors are often aggravated by stress, look for elements in your children's lives that may be causing unhappiness or concern. Are they struggling to keep up with schoolwork? Are their athletic expectations too high? Are your marital problems causing them distress? To reduce the tension your children may be feeling, make yourself more readily available for comfort and assurances and try to eliminate obviously stressful situations. Tic episodes are often reduced in direct proportion to the reduction of stress.

Eliminate Irritants: Some tics begin as a natural reaction to physical irritation. A too-tight or too-high collar can cause head jerking or shrugging; ill-fitting glasses or eyestrain can cause blinking, squinting, or nose wrinkling; hats with chin straps can cause head shaking or nodding; and so on. You can sometimes prevent the tic habit by staying alert to signs of discomfort and by removing the source of irritation.

Consider Nutritional Deficiencies: Many nutritionists believe that persistent tics may be the result of potassium and/or magnesium deficiencies. Potassium and magnesium imbalances are aggravated by sugary diets and the caffeine in chocolates and colas. If you want to take a preventive approach to the tic problem, adjust your children's diet and ask your pediatrician about the advisablity of giving them the over-the-counter diet supplement dolomite, which can replenish the magnesium and potassium they need.

Trigger Identification

Tic behaviors come and go in no predictable pattern. But if you keep a written record for two weeks on the monitoring chart on page 22, you may be able to identify certain kinds of circumstances that trigger tic espisodes. Begin your monitoring during a time period when you expect to be with your children for an extended period (weekends, vacations, or holidays, for example). Mark each tic occurrence on the chart and pay particular attention to the child's activity before and during the tic. This information will aid your efforts to reduce or eliminate tic-aggravating situations.

Self-Awareness

In the majority of cases, children are completely unaware of their tic. Because they cannot stop doing something they don't know they're doing, the first step in breaking the habit is to show your children exactly what they look like during a tic episode. At a time when, according to your monitoring chart, a tic episode is likely, stay with your child in front of a mirror. Together, watch for a tic movement. Imitate the tic with your own body, and then encourage your child to practice the tic movement voluntarily.

Eleven-year-old Randy had a tic habit that caused him to blink and wrinkle his nose forcefully. The habit was most obvious when he was doing schoolwork. One day in the middle of an assignment, his mom brought him to the bathroom mirror and explained that she wanted him to see what he was doing with his eyes and nose. She imitated the squint and in just a few seconds Randy experienced a tic. His mom asked him to describe the action in detail, to relate how it felt, to explain how the muscles tightened and relaxed. They watched for a few more minutes until the tic appeared again. Although class-mates had occasionally laughed at Randy's tic, he was surprised to see and feel himself actually do it.

Every morning, encourage your children to stand in front of the mirror and increase their awareness with an exercise called negative practice. This technique calls for the intentional repetition of the tic, which helps children become more aware of the physical movement involved in their tic. Also, by bringing a previously involuntary behavior under voluntary control, children can learn to control an actual muscle spasm.

Each day Randy would practice his tense blink and nose wrinkling over and over again in rapid succession until the muscles that were involved in his tic became exhausted. This overuse of the involved muscles discouraged the involuntary movement during the day, and the technique improved Randy's ability to recognize the feelings associated with the onset of a tic.

The next step in this awareness stage requires the child to self-monitor tic espisodes. Randy was given his own copy of the monitoring chart and told to put a check on the chart every time he felt himself blink. In the beginning, his mother would often need to point out that he had just blinked, but as the daily mirror awareness exercises made Randy aware of the physical movements involved in his tic, it became easier for him to catch himself blinking.

Awareness and self-monitoring alone can reduce the frequency of tic behaviors. Then as your children become aware of the habit, they can use competing responses to resist the muscle urge leading to tics.

Competing Responses

You can enhance the effectiveness of awareness and monitoring with the following competing responses of alternate activities and relaxation exercises.

Alternate activities teach your children to overcome a tic by substituting a counteracting movement. This technique tenses those muscles that are in direct opposition to those involved in the tic. The following description of specific countermovements can be used for the listed tics, and they also give you an indication of the kind of muscle movement that will counter other tics your children may experience. The relaxation exercises should be practiced daily for fifteen minutes and used again for three minutes anytime you or your child notices a tic.

Eye Blinking: Open the eyes wide and then blink deliberately every five seconds while shifting gaze about every ten seconds.

Head Jerking: Tense the neck muscles while keeping the chin down and in toward the neck. Then press the head against your hand in the opposite direction of the jerking movements.

Grimacing: Slowly tighten the jaw muscles to close the mouth tightly and press the lips together.

Shoulder Jerking: Press the arms tightly against the sides of the body while pulling the shoulders downward; hold that position for a full minute.

Relaxation Exercises: If your children's monitoring chart shows a relationship between stress and tic occurrences, be sure to include relaxation exercises in their daily schedule. When they learn how to control their overall response to tension, you will see a decrease in the frequency and intensity of the tic. The details of three relaxation exercises (thought control, deep breathing, and guided imagery) are explained in Chapter 2. Pick one that suits your child's needs and abilities and use it every day as an important part of this habit-busting program.

Rewards and Penalties

Randy was anxious to get rid of his tic because once he was aware of it, he realized it was hurting his ability to play baseball. But even though Randy was self-motivated, his mom found that she needed something extra to encourage him to keep filling in his self-monitoring chart and doing his negative-practice exercises. You'll probably find that your children, too, need something to push them through to the end of the program.

Randy's mom drew up a progress chart similar to his monitoring chart and gave him a check mark every time he completed his morning exercises, and two check marks at the end of each day if his own chart showed that he had made an effort to keep track of his tic. She promised him that when he had earned twenty checks she would buy him a new baseball glove. She also added a penalty stipulation. Once Randy's mom was certain that Randy was aware of his tics and fully able to feel and record them, she told him she would erase one check on the progress chart every time she noticed an unrecorded blink.

As the program progressed, Randy learned to feel the tic sensation before he actually blinked. Using the alternate activity, he was able to widen his eyes to stop the blink. At the point, Randy's mother erased a progress check every time he experienced his tic without making an effort to stop it. In the beginning Randy lost quite a few checks because he tended to be forgetful. But because he really wanted the new glove, he agreed each night to give it his best effort the following day. Finally, after three weeks, Randy earned his glove and his tic had nearly vanished.

In addition to a reward-and-penalty system, you can promote cooperation with the continuous use of social rewards. Remember to comment positively on any effort or improvement you notice. Note, for example, how smooth your child's face looks without the tic, or how calm he appears without a head or shoulder jerk. Stay attentive for any opportunity to praise and encourage continued cooperation.

If you faithfully practice a tic-busting program that includes daily awareness exercises, a competing-response technique, and a system of rewards and penalties, your child should be relieved of a chronic tic within one month. If the tic shows no sign of improvement, you should not give up. Call your pediatrician and ask for further information about medications that can treat tics, or ask for a referral to a child psychologist trained in hypnosis or biofeedback.

11

Other Common Habits

Lots of children have bad habits. Some repeatedly wrinkle their nose, some pull on their ear, many suck their bottom lip, and others chew on their hair or clothing. The list of childhood bad habits goes on and on, so we cannot possibly cover them all. But by looking specifically at common habits like nose picking, knuckle cracking, finger tapping, foot and leg wiggling, and cheek chewing, this final chapter will show you how almost any bad habit can be broken using the program described in this book.

Habit Prevention

Most habits can be weakened if you catch the behavior as it first becomes repetitive. At that point your goal is to reduce the number of times it's practiced each day; this limits its chance of becoming ingrained. When you see your children practicing the behavior you'd like to discourage, don't call attention to it in negative ways. If your daughter finds that picking her nose will immediately make you yell, "Stop picking your nose!" she's unlikely to stop one of the few things that makes you drop everything to focus on her. Instead, give your attention to times when she's *not* picking. During a TV show, for example, comment, "It's nice to see you watching your show without picking your nose." If you do this often, your child will soon resist picking as a means of getting your attention and approval.

You can also reduce the strength of a habit by continually distracting your child away from it. If, for example, your son cracks his knuckles, without commenting on the practice, throw him a ball, bring him crayons and paper, provide something that will keep his hands busy at times when he's likely to sit and crack.

You can also prevent the formation of bad habits by monitoring your own. Parents who have nervous habits like finger tapping or foot wiggling encourage their children through example to release tension in the same way.

Trigger Identification
Before you tell your children it's time to stop their bad habit, take a full week to watch when, where, and how often they practice the behavior. Use the monitoring chart on page 22 to keep an accurate record. At the end of the week you may find patterns that point out habit triggers such as tension, boredom, fatigue, or even contemplation. This information will tell you when the habit is likely to occur, and it will also guide you in choosing habit-busting methods.

Self-Awareness

Children can't break a habit if they don't see and feel themselves practicing it. Awareness begins with a calm discussion between the two of you. Explain to your child exactly which behavior has become a habit and why it's best to break the habit. Nose picking, for example, is unsanitary; cheek chewing is self-injurious; and knuckle cracking and foot and leg wiggling are disturbing to others. Look for factors that will make it appealing to the child to stop the behavior and then explain the habit-busting program. You'll need your child's cooperation to make the program work, so take as long as necessary to discuss, explain, and motivate.

Next, sit with your children in front of a mirror and tell them to watch themselves practice their habit. Let them see what it is their body is doing and exactly what the habit looks like to other people. Do this mirror exercise every day during the habit-busting program.

Then tell your children that you will help them become aware of their habit by pointing it out each time you see it occurring. In the beginning, children need someone to interrupt the habit because most often they have no idea they're doing it. Your foot wigglers, nose pickers, cheek chewers, and knuckle crackers will be genuinely surprised when you bring the habit to their attention.

Response Prevention

You can weaken a habit by making it impossible to practice. Nose pickers, knuckle crackers, and finger tappers, for example, will find that wearing gloves or mittens completely stops the habit. If your monitoring chart shows that the habit is most often performed in a particular place, like in front of the TV, you might put a pair of mittens next to the TV and instruct your children to put them on every time the set is turned on. Leg wigglers and foot tappers may find their habit less satisfying if they attach a weight to their leg or foot. These tactics are only effective in circumstances when you know the habit is likely to occur.

Competing Response

A competing response is anything that children might do instead of their habit. Your monitoring chart will give you a good indication of what triggers your children's habits and when they're likely to practice them. This information can help you substitute a competing response for the habit. If, for example, you find that your children crack their knuckles in new situations, or pick their nose when doing difficult homework assignments, or chew their cheek when facing a scolding, you'll know that tension is a trigger. To counter this stress response, teach your children to substitute one of the relaxation exercises explained in Chapter 2.

If you notice that the habit is most often practiced while watching TV, or riding in the car, or standing in line, boredom is probably the trigger. In these situations, plan ahead to provide your children with activities that will keep them physically busy and mentally occupied.

The following specific competing responses will give you an idea of how you can also create your own competing response to counter a habit.

Nose Picking: Sit on the hands or put hands in pockets.

Knuckle Cracking: Stretch out the fingers slowly; make a fist and then relax; repeat three times when tempted by a habit or after each habit episode.

Foot/Leg Wiggling: Press the foot flat on the floor; count to five and then relax. Repeat three times.

Finger Tapping: Grab hold of the tabletop and squeeze for thirty seconds. Or make a fist and hold for thirty seconds. Repeat either exercise three times when tempted or after practicing a habit.

Cheek Chewing: Chew gum. Or take several deep breaths with the mouth open.

Rewards and Penalties

Because a bad habit isn't usually very bothersome to young children, most need incentives to break it. That's why rewards and penalties are helpful in guiding children through this program and in helping them succeed. Be sure to post a written progress chart so your children can see when they do well and when they fall behind their goal. Chapter 3 gives you all the information you'll need to use and enforce a successful system of social and concrete rewards as well as penalties. Read it over carefully before you begin your habit-busting program.

Children pick up lots of bad habits. Some will come and go without much notice; some will become the focus of family attention; and some will continue their embarrassing or self-destructive course into adulthood. Your best plan of action is to watch your children carefully when you first notice a bad habit. Without calling undue notice to the behavior, use some preventive strategies that may keep the act from becoming firmly ingrained. But if a bad habit becomes persistent and excessive, don't hesitate to start the habit-busting strategies described in this book. The sooner a habit is addressed, the easier it is to break.

Recommended for further reading for children:
Don't Do That!
Tony Ross
Crown Publishing, 1991

Index

American Academy of Pediatrics, 42
American Health magazine, 65
American Psychiatric Association, 93
American Speech-Language-
  Hearing Foundation, 72, 74
Annoying habits, 7
Attention-getting habits, 4, 34, 57
Awakening, and tooth grinding,
  80–81
Awareness. *See* Self-awareness

Bedtime thumb sucking, 15–16, 39
Behavior
  monitoring, 19–22
  shaping, 11–13
  see also Habit; specific habits
Biofeedback, 84, 101
Bite guard, 81
Bitter-tasting liquids, 42, 53
Boredom, 33, 35, 87, 104
Boys
  stuttering, 67
  tics, 93
Brain
  chemical imbalance in, 55–56
  and stuttering, 66

Breathing. *See* Deep breathing;
  Open-mouth breathing
Bruxism. *See* Teeth grinding

Charts. *See* Habit monitoring chart
Cheek chewing, 103, 105–7
Chewing gum, 39
Chronic tics, 94
Clenching teeth. *See* Teeth
  clenching
Common habits. *See* Habit
Communication system, 15, 88
Competing response, 16–18
  common habits, 106–7
  hair pulling, 61–62
  masturbation, 89–90
  nail biting, 50–51
  stuttering, 73
  teeth grinding, 79–80
  thumb sucking, 39–40
  tics, 99–100
Compliments, 10
Concrete rewards, 26–28, 107
Consistency of enforcement, 29–30
Criticism, and social rewards, 25

Deep breathing, 18–19
Disciplinary tactics, 28–29

Disfluency. *See* Stuttering
Dodes, John, 76

Elbow splint, 15–16, 38, 60–61
Embarrassment, 5–6, 54, 86, 91
Enforcement guidelines, 29–30
Exercises, relaxation. *See*
    Relaxation exercises
Eye blinking, 99

Fatigue, 35, 104
Finger sucking. *See* Thumb sucking
Finger tapping, 103, 107
Fluency shaping, 73
Foot wiggling, 103, 105–7
Friends, 9–10

Gender. *See* Boys; Girls
Genetic predisposition
    stuttering, 67
    teeth grinding, 76
    tics, 94
Genital touching. *See* Masturbation
Girls, and hair pulling, 56
Gloves, 39, 50, 61, 105
Goal setting, 12
Grab bag, 26
Grimacing, 99
Grinding. *See* Teeth grinding
Guided imagery, 19, 40, 79
Gum, as thumb-sucking substitute,
    39

Habit, 1–10, 103–8
    definition, 2

    reasons for breaking, 5–8
    as response to nervousness,
        16–17, 47, 51
    as response to tension, 3–4
    roots of formation, 2–5
    see also specific habits
Habit-busting strategies, 11–22
    for common habits, 104–8
    for hair pulling, 58–63
    interest boosters, 23–30
    for masturbation, 87–91
    modeling for, 8–9
    for nail biting, 47–54
    public commitment for, 9–10
    for stuttering, 72–74
    support for, 10
    for teeth grinding, 77–84
    for thumb sucking, 36–40
    for tics, 97–101
Habit monitoring chart, 19–22
    for common habits, 104
    filling in, 21–22
    for hair pulling, 58, 62–63
    for masturbation, 87
    for nail biting, 47–48, 52–53
    sample, 22
    for teeth grinding, 77–78, 82, 83
    for thumb sucking, 37
    for tics, 97, 100
Habit prevention
    common habits, 103–4
    hair pulling, 56–58
    masturbation, 86
    nail biting, 46–47

stuttering, 68–70
teeth grinding, 76–77
thumb sucking, 32–34
tics, 95–96
Hair pulling, 6–7, 55–63
Hands, 50–51, 57, 61, 104
    see also Finger tapping;
    Knuckle cracking; Nail biting;
    Thumb sucking
Head jerking, 5, 99
Hypnosis, 84, 101

Imitation, 3, 8–9, 46, 94
Infants
    and teeth grinding, 76–77
    and thumb sucking, 32–33
Insecurity, 35
Interest boosters, 23–30
Irritants, physical, 96

Jaw problems, 75, 78

Knuckle cracking, 103–8

Learning by imitation. *See*
    Modeling
Leg wiggling, 103, 105–7

Magnesium deficiency, 96
Manicures, 46, 49–50
Masturbation, 13, 85–91
Modeling, 8–9
Monitoring chart. *See* Habit
    monitoring chart

Motivations, habit-breaking, 8–10
    see also Rewards

Nail biting, 8–9, 12, 45–54
National Council Against Health
    Fraud, The, 76
Negative reinforcement, 4, 28–29, 34
Nervous habit, 16–17, 47, 51
"Nervous tic", 95
Nose picking, 103–6
Nutritional deficiencies, 96

Obsessive-compulsive disorders, 55
Open-mouth breathing, 79, 83
Oral addiction, 39

Pacifier, 32–33
Parents
    with nervous habits, 104
    as role models, 8–9, 46
Pattern, habit behavior, 20
Penalties
    for common habits, 107–8
    as disciplinary tactic, 28–29
    for hair pulling, 62–63
    for masturbation, 90–91
    for nail biting, 52–53
    for teeth grinding, 81–82
    for thumb sucking, 29, 41–42
    for tics, 100–1
Penis-holding. *See* Masturbation
Personality disorders, 5
Physical irritants, 96
Positive reinforcement, 2, 4, 23–28

Potassium deficiency, 96
Praise, 25, 46
Preschoolers' thumb sucking, 34–36
Privileges, 26–27
Public commitment, 9–10
Punishment. *See* Penalties

Rapid eye movement (REM) sleep, 80–81
Relaxation exercises, 17–19
  for hair pulling, 62–63
  for masturbation, 89
  for nail biting, 51
  for teeth grinding, 79, 80, 82, 83
  for thumb sucking, 40
  for tic control, 99–100
Response, competing. *See* Competing response
Response prevention, 15–16
  for common habits, 105–6
  for hair pulling, 60–61
  for masturbation, 89
  for nail biting, 50
  for stuttering, 73–74
  for teeth grinding, 81
  for thumb sucking, 38–39
Rewards, 23–28
  concrete, 26–28, 107
  evaluating, 28
  social, 24–26, 63, 82, 101, 107
  to counter common habits, 107–8
  to counter hair pulling, 62–63
  to counter masturbation, 90–91
  to counter nail biting, 52–53

  to counter teeth grinding, 81–82
  to counter thumb sucking, 27–28, 35–36, 41
  to counter tics, 100–1
Ridicule, 5
Rubber-band therapy, 53

Self-awareness, 14–15
  of common habits, 105
  of hair pulling, 59–60
  of masturbation, 88
  of nail biting, 48–50
  of stuttering, 73
  of teeth grinding, 78
  of thumb sucking, 14–15, 38
  of tics, 97–98
Self-touching. *See* Masturbation
Shaping, 11–13, 73
Shoulder jerking, 99
Sleep
  and teeth grinding, 79, 80–81
  and thumb sucking, 15–16, 39
Social rewards, 24–26, 63, 82, 101, 107
Sonograms, 32
Speech disfluency. *See* Stuttering
Speech Foundation of America, 65, 71, 72, 74
Speech pathologist, 70–72
Splinting, elbow, 15–16, 38, 60–61
Stopzit®, 42
Stress
  and common habits, 2, 3–4, 104, 106

and hair pulling, 59, 62
and nail biting, 47, 51
relaxation techniques, 16–19
and stuttering, 67
and teeth grinding, 78, 79, 82–83
and thumb sucking, 40
and tics, 95, 96, 99–100
Stuttering, 65–74
  boys and, 67
  causes for, 66–67
  common versus at-risk, 71
  management strategies, 68–70
  speech pathologist for, 70–72
Sucking instinct, 32–33
Supportiveness, from parents, 10,
  46–47, 57–58

Teeth
  clenching, 76, 77–78, 83
  grinding, 15, 75–84
  thumb-sucking effect on, 33
Temporomandibular disorders
  (TMJ), 75
Tension. See Stress
Thought control

as stress response, 17–18
for thumb sucking, 40
Thumb sucking, 5, 20, 31–43
  by toddlers, 33–34
  nighttime, 15–16, 39
  as trigger for hair pulling, 59
Tics, 5–6, 93–101
  boys and, 93
  causes, 94–95
TMJ. See Temporomandibular
  disorders
Tongue depressor, 15–16, 38,
  60–61
Tourette's syndrome, 95
Transient tics, 93–94
Trichotillomania. See Hair pulling
Trigger identification, 13, 20
  common habits, 104
  hair pulling, 58–59
  masturbation, 13, 87
  nail biting, 47–48
  stuttering, 73
  teeth grinding, 77–78
  thumb sucking, 37
  tics, 97

About the Authors

DR. CHARLES E. SCHAEFER, Ph.D., is Professor of Psychology at Fairleigh Dickinson University in New Jersey as well as the Director of its Crying Baby Clinic. He has written twenty-five books on various aspects of child psychology.

THERESA FOY DiGERONIMO, M.Ed., is an author specializing in child-care issues and is the mother of three children. She has written five books with Dr. Schaefer.